Praise for *Lenses of Humanity*

"Through compelling personal stories and profound, timeless principles, Kyle encourages us to live up to our humanity by knowing ourselves, enhancing our relationship with others, demonstrating layers of empathy, and creating positive communities. By seeing and acting with humanity through these four lenses, we can be safe, become, belong, and believe. These human yearnings apply to family, work, neighborhood, education, and church settings. The right book for our time."

—DAVE ULRICH, Rensis Likert Professor,
Ross School of Business, University of Michigan;
partner, The RBL Group; best-selling author

Lenses
of
Humanity

HOW REFLECTION, CONNECTION, AND EMPATHY CAN HEAL OUR WORLD

KYLE A. REYES, PhD

RIVER GROVE
BOOKS

Published by River Grove Books
Austin, TX
www.rivergrovebooks.com

Distributed by River Grove Books

Design and composition by Greenleaf Book Group
Cover design by Greenleaf Book Group

Publisher's Cataloging-in-Publication data is available.

Print ISBN: 978-1-63299-884-2

eBook ISBN: 978-1-63299-885-9

First Edition

To my dear Michele, my kids, my parents, and my siblings,
thank you for your love.

Contents

PART 1 The Inner Lens: Humanity-driven people engage in ongoing self-analysis, reflection, and lens-checking

PART 2 The Context Lens: Humanity-driven people study and engage with diversity of history, thought, and perspective

PART 3 The Empathy Lens: Humanity-driven people learn from and improve empathy for diverse individuals

My Lenses and My Why

I AM A FORMER COLLEGE DROPOUT TURNED EDUCATOR and a graffiti artist turned shoe designer. As a son of a Hawaiian Japanese mother who was a high school administrator in the Los Angeles Unified School District for forty years and a Filipino immigrant father who was a visual and performing artist, it's easy to see where these passions for education and art are rooted. Since 2003, I have worked in higher education as a staff member, faculty member, and administrator. Throughout my career, I have focused on improving the learning and working experiences of the students and employees I serve—with an eye to their unique and diverse needs. I have taught cross-cultural communication, multicultural understanding, English language learner methodologies, and various courses exploring cross-cultural understanding. I have spoken to or consulted with over three hundred organizations in over thirty states on cultural competence, strategic inclusion planning, intercultural communication, and other topics regarding individual and organizational commitment to human diversity and dignity.

My lenses have been shaped by a story that is becoming increasingly familiar—individuals from mixed identity (religious, linguistic, racial/ethnic) backgrounds navigating the world to find a sense of connection, relevancy, and contribution. But I also recognize that one does not need a "mixed" background to understand the complexity of finding our place in the world and our contribution to it. Many of the stories in this book come from my experiences. This text is part memoir, part academic investigation, and part public discourse. It stems from my personal, messy journey. It has taken shape through my ups and downs as an educator, artist, community advocate, and family man.

During the writing process, one of the publishing consultants asked me "Who is your audience?" It wasn't the first time I had received that question, but I felt like I needed to produce a specific answer better than "I hope everyone." Over the next two days, my audience became clearer to me. My audience is my children. More than anything, I wanted to write a book that would be a consistent life message to them to be kind people. To be bridge builders. To show up in life with a desire to learn from others and be excited to engage with diverse people and perspectives. I wanted them to know what I have dedicated my life to—making connections with people to communicate their value. One day, when I have passed on, I want my children and grandchildren to know that I don't care what profession they choose, how much money they make, or what titles they have. I just want them to be good humans—people who treat other humans with respect and dignity. I want them to put good into the world. And I think this book can help them do that. Thank you for trusting me with your time and for finding out how you can develop the lenses and actions needed to build humanity.

Introduction

"One way or another, we all have to find what best
fosters the flowering of our humanity in this
contemporary life and dedicate ourselves to that."

—JOSEPH CAMPBELL

IN THE SPRING OF 2007, at the age of thirty, I recognized that my
vision was becoming quite blurry. I decided to visit an optometrist
for the first time in a long time. She ran me through a series of
minor tests, including staring at a green dot, waiting for a puff of air
to blast my eye, and finally, doing my best to read letters off a
chart. The first line of letters was easy, but as the font size shrank
with each new line, I found my confidence waning in discerning
between an "O," a "C," and a "G." The doctor gave me no indicators
that I had ever erred, but she periodically switched the lenses of
the phoropter. With each lens switch, the smaller letters became
clearer. And shortly after rattling off the letters on the smallest line,
I received a set of test glasses for my prescription. It was amazing:
what was once blurry was now incredibly clear.

Five years later, as I was completing my doctoral dissertation, I
found that objects about fifteen feet away were fuzzy and objects
thirty feet away were getting blurry, even with my glasses on. I

returned to the same optometrist and asked her, in a snarky tone, "Just curious, why do I have to get another prescription? I paid a lot of money for these glasses, and I thought they were supposed to last longer than this." She paused, then smiled and said, "Yeah . . . there's a term for what you're experiencing . . . *age*." We laughed and then she said something that would have a significant impact on my life and career. She said, "Kyle, your lenses have been shifting this entire time without you knowing it." She then continued to explain that such shifts would continue subtly and slowly for the rest of my life.

Since that day, the metaphor of *lens shifting* has become a focus of mine. The notion that our physical, visual lenses can shift without our conscious awareness suggests that such shifts in our psychological lenses warrant attention as well—especially as we consider our relationships and interactions with one another. I hope to remind us of the need for intentional lens development as we address an erosion of humanity.

Why Humanity?

We live in an era when tensions in every sector of our lives are high. You can feel it everywhere you go. Amid political divisiveness, global pandemics, volatile markets, culture wars, and social media echo chambers, there is ample evidence that our individual and collective humanity has waned.

Humans are suffering. Pervasive poverty, abuse, suicidal ideation, war, starvation, stress, fear, and isolation are overwhelming. These maladies are exacerbated by our decreasing ability to engage positively across differences, demonstrate empathy for opposing views, and seek understanding through civility. The phrase "I have lost my faith in humanity" is commonplace in response to tragic shootings, civil unrest, demonizing of political opponents, human trafficking, and genocide. If you're reading this book, you're probably tired, like I am, of the negativity.

At its core, humanity is about human understanding, connection, and dignity. It's about recognizing that we are complex, thoughtful, and diverse. Increasingly, we view one another's differences as threats, and our natural fight-or-flight response limits our ability to develop new understandings, relationships, and lenses. How, then, do we address this erosion of humanity, and can we even make a difference as individuals? The answers to these two questions formulate the focus of this book. Through a research-informed, story-filled journey, I offer an aspirational and practical approach to reclaiming our humanity.

Intentionally Reengaging Our Humanity: A New Framework

For nearly fifteen years, I have researched humanity, cultural competence, intercultural communication, and related concepts. Included in this research are years of practical implementation in academia, in the community, and through hundreds of consultations across the United States. My research and community work have also revealed the need to examine prevailing and often ineffective approaches to what I refer to as "checkbox" diversity work—or work that only treats issues of cultural competence as mandatory training to check off.

The important work of cultural understanding has been nested in thorny political agendas that often don't invite healthy exchange. Rather than feed into the political divide, I present an approach that prioritizes humanity. The framework and structure of this book are born from my belief in lens development as a deliberate effort to see things anew—and when we see things anew, our behavior follows.

Personal growth and transformation come from honest reflection and self-analysis. I agree with John Dewey's sentiment that we don't learn from our experiences alone. Rather, true growth and learning come from reflection on our experiences.[1] In this book, I invite you to embrace the messiness of human nuance and complexity. Only through the messiness do we become more competent in showing up for one another with greater humanity.

The following framework provides a visual model of the substance of this book and a new way to understand the connections found within. The table shows two sets of variables. On the x-axis, the two columns (Individual and Collective) demonstrate the level at which the work occurs. This distinction is important, as humanity requires work unique to the individual and the collective. The y-axis focuses on where the work or efforts must be directed (Inward and Outward). The direction of our efforts helps us manage the work that needs to be done internally and externally.

QUADRANT 1: WORKING INWARD AT THE INDIVIDUAL LEVEL = INNER LENS

The Inner Lens focuses on the work we need to do to unpack our stuff—exploring how and why we view the world the way we do—and why it matters regarding how we show up for others.

QUADRANT 2: WORKING INWARD AT THE COLLECTIVE LEVEL = CONTEXT LENS

The Context Lens challenges us to do the work of deliberate and contextual learning to situate every interaction in a more holistic understanding and interpretation.

QUADRANT 3: WORKING OUTWARD AT THE INDIVIDUAL LEVEL = EMPATHY LENS

The Empathy Lens teaches us the power of humanizing communication and engagement in one-to-one interactions and relationships.

QUADRANT 4: WORKING OUTWARD AT THE COLLECTIVE LEVEL = COMMUNITY LENS

The Community Lens reframes our commitment to enhancing humanity among the groups and communities we are a part of.

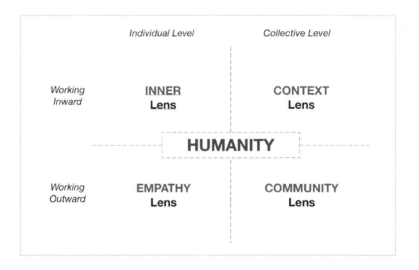

As we assess our efforts and map what we can do to develop each of the four lenses of humanity, this table can help us organize our thoughts and remember the direction and level of our efforts.

After reading this book, you will not only have a deeper understanding of each lens but also a set of activities and next steps to develop these lenses actively and intentionally. Furthermore, I also encourage you to visit my Instagram page @lensesofhumanity where I post the artwork and other images mentioned throughout this book. Through this lens development, you can build community, improve relationships, and develop a stronger sense of purpose and value.

The Lenses of Humanity and Our Quest for Stability, Connection, and Purpose

After one of my presentations in Boston, a woman approached me, thanked me for my remarks, and asked if I had a few minutes to talk after I gathered my things. I agreed to chat, and after visiting with a few more people, I packed up my laptop and went to the hall to meet her. When I turned the corner, I noticed her eyes were red from crying, and she had a tissue in her hand. She breathed in and out a few times and then told me why she was so emotional. She shared that some key relationships (friends and family) had suffered because certain topics had become too toxic and divisive for healthy conversation. She then discussed how the lenses of humanity framework I spoke about provided her with concrete ways to try to mend relationships and show up for her loved ones in healthier ways— even across lines of disagreement. As I have shared iterations of this model and the adjoining concrete action steps, I have heard many similar stories from people who felt that they finally had an optimistic and humanity-driven approach to engaging with and navigating a divisive and polarized world.

Various surveys and studies have explored people's needs—what they crave, what they desire, and what motivates them. In the famed Harvard Study of Adult Development, Robert Waldinger reported one of the key findings: "Good relationships keep us happier and healthier. Period."[2]

My own research and meta-study align with the Harvard Study. Over the course of four years, and in an effort to understand human connection, nuance, and motivation, I conducted focus groups and did an analysis of scores of other studies to address this question: If I were to lift humanity, what areas of the human experience could I impact? My findings and the synthesis of additional studies suggest that across culture, age, gender, and other identifiers, humans yearn for three things: (1) stability and safety, (2) meaningful connection with other humans, and (3) a sense of purpose and meaning.

The following table represents the words and concepts that emerged from my focus groups as the most powerful human yearnings. These words also affect our understanding of what it means to be human.

WORDS MOST ASSOCIATED WITH HUMAN YEARNING

Safety and Stability	Connection and Belonging	Purpose and Meaning
• Security	• Relationships	• Achievement
• Basic needs (food, water, air, sleep, shelter)	• Community	• Recognition
• Peace	• Intimacy	• Respect
• Comfort	• Friendship	• Value
• Freedom	• Trust	• Growth
• Autonomy	• Love	• Development
	• Validation	• Relevance
	• Understanding	• Potential

As you review the words in the three columns, do any of them resonate with you regarding what you most yearn for in life? What's missing? It is important to assess our understanding of these lists because, if they truly capture what we, as humans, yearn for, **the quest to improve our humanity begins with a desire to bring about these things for others. If we can help people experience safety and stability, connection and belonging, and purpose and meaning, we are facilitating greater humanity.** We are dignifying the human experience, and this book helps us do that.

> If we can help people experience safety and stability, connection and belonging, and purpose and meaning, we are facilitating greater humanity.

I have found the people I consider to be most humanity-driven in my life are regularly helping other people in at least one of these three human-yearning dimensions. So, how do we become one of those people? How do we live in a more humanity-driven way? What can we do today to improve humanity?

I invite you on this journey to answer these questions and many more. No matter our backgrounds, education, or experiences, we can all be more deliberate in living our lives with greater humanity. And there is no doubt that our world needs this now more than ever.

PART 1

The Inner Lens

Humanity-driven people engage in ongoing self-analysis, reflection, and lens-checking

Inner Lens Snapshot

As humanity-driven people, we seek to understand how our brains receive and organize information. This is the foundation to more fully understand how and why we see what we see and do what we do. We become more aware and conscious of our brain functions and how such functions affect our perspectives and behaviors. We are honest with ourselves, take ownership of our biases, and develop an openness to change. We set aside time for personal reflection and proactively check our lenses, allowing us to become more intentional about our thoughts, attitudes, and actions—especially as we think about our engagement with others.

Why an Inner Lens?

Any type of cultural learning or learning about differences begins by looking inward. We must first understand ourselves if we are to be more aware of the filters we use to interpret and then engage with others.

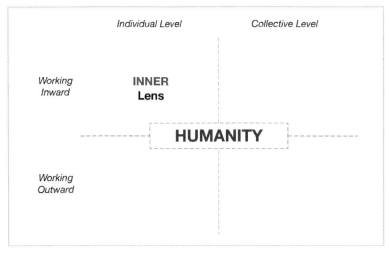

Lenses of Humanity Framework: Inner Lens Focus

CHAPTER 1

Librarian of the Mind: Explore the Stuff in Your Brain

"Your vision will become clear only when you look into your own heart. Who looks outside, dreams; who looks inside, awakens."

—CARL JUNG

IN JANUARY 2017, I sat in a delivery room with my wife, Michele, awaiting the birth of our youngest child. The nurses, as they had done with our previous deliveries, provided us with a folder of informational pamphlets often given to parents admitted for delivery. One of the documents, titled "Skin-to-Skin Contact," outlined research on the importance of the first skin connection between baby and mother—especially if the mother was planning on nursing. The pamphlet read, "Recent research has shown that the first hours after childbirth is an unparalleled time for bonding between mother and baby."[1] The nurses explained the skin-to-skin protocols. Historically, after the umbilical cord was cut, the nurses took the naked newborn to the warming station. They checked vitals, cleaned and swaddled the baby, and brought the child back to the mother. Now, the nurses, with their rubber gloves on, immediately place the newborn on the mother, chest-to-chest, for a skin-to-skin connection within those vital first moments.

At 10:21 a.m., our daughter, Anuhea (ah-noo-hay-uh), was born. I cut the umbilical cord. The nurses placed our crying daughter on Michele's upper chest. As soon as Anuhea was laid on her mother, Michele caressed her and spoke to her. What happened next remains a remarkable memory for me. Anuhea quieted down as Michele spoke, and a short time later, our baby girl latched on to her mother to nurse for the first time. A connection between mother and daughter had indeed taken place.

Childhood Coding

One of the most significant influences on why we do what we do is also one of the most minuscule. We are born with billions of neurons. As we develop cognitively, engage with the world around us, and have life experiences, these neurons interact through synaptic connections, and information is processed or coded along our neurological pathways. This process begins in the womb, and by the time babies are born, they possess astounding cognitive abilities. According to the Urban Child Institute:

> Newborns can recognize human faces, which they prefer over other objects, and can even discriminate between happy and sad expressions. At birth, a baby knows her mother's voice and may be able to recognize the sounds of stories her mother read to her while she was still in the womb.[2]

When Anuhea was born and no longer in the warmth and comfort of the womb, she began to cry. It was a jarring, new experience she didn't like. As she tried to open her eyes, she quickly shut them due to light that she had not encountered previously. Her natural systems kicked in to protect her from discomfort. And then, when Michele spoke to her, she found something that signaled to her brain, "This is familiar; this is comforting." Even though Anuhea did not have the foundational or anchoring synapses to process some of the new data (like lights or the English language), she quieted down when she heard her mother's voice.

There is something profound about how early we all begin to navigate the world around us and process our place in it. As our nervous system continues to form, we develop a fundamental code of safety. It is a unique system that we develop early on, programmed to keep us from harm. In the first years of our lives, we gather information at an incredible rate through our various senses and the rapid development of our synapses. We become social scientists at a very early age. We begin coding connections regarding love, belonging, intellect, talent, community, and sense of place. We may not be able to name such feelings for many years, but we can sense them. And every time something happens, and we receive neural signals of our feelings associated with the incident, we expand the map in our brains of our place in the world. Knowing these systems are a part of our human survival, we can have empathy for ourselves and others.

Synaptic codes are strengthened or broken based on the frequency and intensity of experiences. If we touch something hot and it barely hurts us, we register immediate pain and discomfort, but the code might not be strong. If we touch something hot again and it burns us more intensely, it becomes a stronger code in our brains. Then add the auditory processing of a parent or guardian telling us not to touch certain things because they are hot. Or the visual coding when we see that metal objects turn orange or red when heated. Over time, our collective experiences with hot objects create truths in our minds—we do not want to touch and get burned by things that give us certain cues. And we instinctively ensure that we are careful around, or stay away from, such dangerous experiences. Our subconscious survival instinct and our conscious database affect our behavior.

We see similar results if we extend the example of hot objects to any social setting. When we are teased or made fun of, it may not hurt the first time too much, or at least it may not get coded strongly in our minds. If such experiences are repeated (frequency) or escalated (intensity), the coding strengthens, and our behavior shifts to survival mode and seeking safety.

Have you ever observed a young person (perhaps your child) whose behavior changed suddenly due to an experience with friends or at school? They decide to stay away from or be careful around the things or people that could hurt them. You may recall your own experiences on the receiving end of unkindness. We may shut down in certain situations because of the codes developed through such experiences. We may avoid certain spaces altogether because of the intensity of previous encounters. Conversely, we might feel empowered to take on new challenges if our previous experiences have warranted loving, encouraging, and hopeful validation. The negative codes (fear of pain) and positive codes (confidence from validation) are heavily influenced by the people in our lives and the places where their influence is most impactful.

The institutions that are most formative regarding our early navigation of life and the codes we develop are family and school.

Theoretically, these institutions should be where people feel safest, most validated, and loved. In some cases this is true, but often these are the very spaces where trust, confidence, and love are broken. These institutions have the greatest influence on our early code development because (1) they are the places where we spend the most time, especially in our formative years, and (2) we assume inherent trust in these institutions and the people who represent them.

In these institutions, we are exposed to our first authority figures, or people we look to for answers. At home, we naturally seek approval, affection, and validation from our parents or guardians. We formulate part of our worth and value at school through academic performance and relationships with teachers and peers.

If we do not feel safe at home or school, why would we want to spend time there or engage with the people who run those institutions? Our families, our schooling, and other life experiences influence how we negotiate with one another, cope with adversity, learn to share, process emotions, believe in things, learn social cues, develop traditions, problem-solve, deal with the abstract, understand consequences, develop tastes and preferences, and formulate a sense of purpose, value, and identity. Later, as we grow and mature, our work environment also influences our sense of place and value. Just think about your own life and social settings right now. What codes have you carried with you since childhood? How does your behavior change around certain people because of past experiences? We are all social scientists trying to find our sense of safety, connection, and purpose. Yet, we forget that some codes have been with us since we were little.

Over time and with enough experience, the codes in our minds move from randomly placed Post-it Notes to organized categories, referred to as *schemata*. These schemata are the default categories our minds have unconsciously created that help organize information for easy access. This is important for efficient and informed decision-making and choosing the best possible option for survival and comfort. In some ways, our brains are like libraries filled with card catalogs or schema boxes. We have collected cards about everything we see, hear, do, and experience. The danger is not in the existence of the schemata (boxes) or the synapses (individual cards of information). The danger is failing to evaluate or reconsider what we passively gather.

Just think about your own life and social settings right now. What codes have you carried with you since childhood?

In the development of your mind's library, who is the librarian? Who controls what cards are put there? We need to become aware of how often the cards influence how we perceive and act toward one another.

Passive vs. Active Cataloging

In my consulting work, I often ask people about first impressions and stereotypes. I invite them to be honest about images and feelings that come to them when certain labels or terms are used. Let's try it now. When you read a particular word, an image of a person will come to your mind immediately. Don't overthink it. Just be honest about the gender, race, and overall appearance of the person who comes to mind when you read certain words.

- *Surgeon.* What type of person came to your mind? Why do you think that image immediately came to your mind?

- *Pastor.* Again, be honest about the type of person who came to mind.

- *Elementary teacher*. Did a specific teacher come to mind? Remember, there is no right answer. Depending on your lived experiences, your image will differ from others.

- *Terrorist*. What image arrived this time? What gender? What race or ethnicity?

These follow-up questions have led to very interesting conversations. I have conducted this exercise for nearly a decade and have a sound sample size of responses. The one word that elicits the most consistent responses from most participants is *terrorist*. Let's explore this a bit more.

When asked about the image that came to their minds when I said the word *terrorist*, most participants[3] (although hesitant at first) said that an image of a Middle Eastern male came to their minds. In most groupings, the range is from 80 to 90 percent of the participants with this same response. The identity with the second highest rate is that of a white male. Virtually no one had an image of a female come to mind. Why is this? When asked why they thought that particular image came to their minds, most participants said that an image of Osama bin Laden is mentally tied to the word *terrorist* because of the September 11, 2001 attacks. This exercise reveals a concerning collective bias, which is not the most critical finding.

After the conversation, I then ask participants to mentally retrieve their card catalog box labeled *Middle Eastern men*. I invite you to do the same. As you assess the cards of information in that box, what percentage have a positive connotation or association? I typically ask, "How many of you have a majority of the cards—at least 51 percent—with a positive association?" I invite the group to be honest about the information they have gathered regarding Middle Eastern men over their lifetimes. In most groups, around 10 to 15 percent raise their hands. I then ask these individuals, "Where do those positive cards come from?" And every time, I receive a variety of answers, including the following:

- I am married to . . .
- I have a relative who is . . .
- I have a dear friend who is . . .
- I have taken classes about . . .
- I have visited . . .
- I have read books about . . .
- My father-in-law is . . .
- I have students who are from . . .
- I am . . .

These answers highlight a common thread of exposure, connection, and meaningful engagement. In most cases, the individuals put the cards in their mental boxes proactively and intentionally. But what about those who didn't have the majority of cards about Middle Eastern men positively associated? Do I believe these are the truly racist or sexist among us? No. But herein lies the problem and where we encounter the more significant finding. Most cards in our mental boxes are passively or subconsciously collected and are never questioned or examined.

I was fascinated by how passive the process was for the stereotype to enter the mental card catalogs of so many individuals—including mine. It is not as if every group had an option to proactively associate the word *terrorist* with any number of identities. Imagine gathering with your friends around a table with cards labeled with different identities. You then collectively choose a label like *terrorist* and decide to proactively code your brains to associate *terrorist* with Middle Eastern men. We would never do this, because the exercise would be absurd and overtly racist and sexist. And yet, our casual consumption of information has a powerful influence on the cards that enter our schemata or mental boxes. Our brains are such efficient machines that we often don't realize how much the auto-cataloging has been set up for our comfort and safety. The desire to develop stronger lenses of humanity prompts us to become more aware of what is in our brains and what we can do to intentionally develop new codes with new cards. We need to challenge the auto-cataloging of information and curate more carefully the information we are gathering.

Becoming a Librarian of Your Mind

How many of the cards in your mental boxes have been actively put there by you? If you studied and learned a second language, those cards were purposely put there by you. If you learned how to cook from someone in your family, the skill cards you earned were actively put there by your efforts. When you read a book of your choice or attend a seminar you registered for, you are intentionally seeking out new information cards to put in your brain. But not all cards were actively and intentionally acquired. Or, a card was received without context.

While we think we are in control of what goes into our brains, most of the cards in our mental boxes have been received passively. Our brain's natural process takes loads of information every second, only to file it away for efficient retrieval. We process ten to eleven billion bits of information per second but can only cognitively process thirty to sixty bits for conscious navigation. Remember, our neurological computers, in their best efforts to help us navigate life, are also the reason we hold hidden assumptions, prejudices, and biases. Our mental codes are formed through repetition and intensity of information gathered.

If something gets repeated, even if we don't agree with it or it isn't true, it holds space in our mental boxes as a possibility. This recognition of the power of passive card-collecting should awaken us to the dangers of biased codes. Advertising and marketing agencies feed off this psychological dynamic. Scores of marketing and consumer behavior studies have shown the effectiveness of jingles and celebrity voices (auditory cues), packaging and placement (visual cues), lifestyle improvements (emotional cues), and flavor enhancements (taste cues). We attribute positive or negative values to each card as we gather experiences based on these cues. Such attribution influences our future decision-making to reinforce the positive and limit the negative. This doesn't sound bad when deciding what foods to buy and what concert we prefer to go to, but this process also impacts how we view and interact with others.

The same coding through passive card collecting holds true for how media can frame our perceptions of people who are different than us. Remember the discussion of Middle Eastern men? In 2017, Caroline Mala Corbin's research addressed this collective marketing bias.[4] Through her analysis of media clips, news articles, press conferences, and other media sources, she found that the collective media represented "terrorists as always (brown) Muslims." The frequency (repetition of a message) and intensity (emotional reaction or connection) of messaging can have significant and lasting effects on the human brain, behavior, and relations.

If we do not take out the mental boxes regularly to assess what cards have been gathered, we become passive consumers of the messages others want us to have. To appreciate the diversity of humanity, we need to understand that such diversity has already been cataloged in our minds in mostly passive ways. We must become better librarians of our mental card catalogs. We are responsible for knowing what and how information enters our minds and how much value, weight, and significance we give it. When books are donated to a library, the librarian doesn't simply accept all the books and put them out on the shelves. They review the books to assess their condition and overall contribution to the library. They actively inventory what goes on the shelves and what cards are created. This proactive analysis is a critical component of developing the Inner Lens of Humanity.

CHAPTER SUMMARY

- From birth, we gather data about the world and our place in it. These data are coded in our brains in very powerful ways, and they affect our behavior. The higher the frequency and intensity of the inputs, the more powerful the coding in our brains about the world around us.

- Over time, the data points (information) we gather or are exposed to are organized into schemata or categories to help us navigate life to maximize efficiency and ensure safety and comfort.

- The schemata are like card catalog boxes in the libraries of our minds. These boxes hold the information we have processed, with most information received passively.

- We need to become more active and deliberate librarians about the information in our brains and how such information affects our daily attitudes, perspectives, and behavior.

CHAPTER 2

Baseball and Cricket: Learn What You Know and How You Know It

"It is impossible for a man to learn what he thinks he already knows."

—EPICTETUS

IN 2014, I HAD THE PRIVILEGE of visiting New Zealand to set up a teaching experience for my students. The days were full of engagement with Māori immersion schools as possible sites for student teaching. After a full day of meetings and visits, I returned to my hotel and turned on the TV to browse local sports. All five sports channels showed either rugby or cricket. Having some understanding of rugby, I thought I would learn something new and tuned in to a cricket match. I made it a point to pay close attention, hoping that my understanding of baseball would provide some basis for comprehending the game of cricket.

After two hours of watching and listening to the cricket

commentary, I was sure that I knew less about the game than I did when I started watching. I knew that the game was popular in many countries worldwide, and even the most popular sport in some, so I was determined to learn more about it. The next night, I resumed watching another match. Yet I was still unable to grasp the game's core rhythms and subtle nuances.

I compare that experience to watching the 2020 World Series. As a Southern California kid, I was excited to see that my Dodgers were in the World Series for the third time in four years—though they had not won since 1988. I watched all six epic games against the Tampa Bay Rays. Throughout the series, I analyzed the managers' moves and the game within the game. I knew exactly why a pitcher was brought in against a certain batter. I knew what a shift was and why it was on. I questioned certain decisions due to the batter's averages in similar situations. I studied the game-to-game decisions regarding the rotation of starters and relievers. I appreciated small ball in some games and power ball in others. I understood how pitch count in the first game would affect the fourth and fifth games. And so much more.

I understand if you read the paragraph about cricket and laughed. I also understand if you read the baseball paragraph and had no idea what I was talking about. Congratulations if you "get" both cricket and baseball on deep levels. So why the sports stories? Much of what we know about things we can't explain. When we gather information cards about something, they get filed away in our mental boxes. We have the knowledge, but many times we don't know how we know what we know, and we don't know how and why other people don't know.

My mental box labeled *baseball* has many cards. I played baseball in Little League and high school. I collected baseball cards and worked at a sports card shop in high school. I have watched the Dodgers my whole life. I watch analysts talk about baseball. I then watch reruns of the same people saying the same things about baseball. I watch highlights. I talk to other baseball geeks who have played, watched, and analyzed the game. In short, I am a baseball nerd. But one thing I have never done is sit down and study the official rules of baseball.

Written and Unwritten Rules

In baseball, all runners go on a 3–2 count with two outs. How do I know the written rules as well as the unwritten rules? Exposure and engagement opportunities. I have had multiple opportunities to observe and participate in baseball-related activities, and I've had coaches along the way. Through these experiences, I have learned the general rules as well as the hidden rules of the game. Because of this exposure, I might assume that every other person has had similar opportunities and just did not take advantage of them. My natural assumption might be that it's their fault they don't know the rules. This assumption fails to acknowledge that not everyone gets the same opportunities for exposure to my same life experiences, and my judgment about them is quick, ill-informed, and limited based on the cards in my head. I would be frustrated if the same assumption was made about me based on my lack of exposure to something in particular. I affix a high value to baseball and might judge those who don't know as much about it. I imagine those with the same level of exposure to and engagement with cricket might feel the same way.

Part of my frustration with understanding cricket was how much I tried to fit it into my baseball framework. I was trying to layer my interpretation of cricket over a rigid foundation of base-ball, which blocked my ability to learn. Ultimately, I decided it must not be good if it doesn't make sense to me. People refer to various new experiences, saying, "I don't get it. It's stupid." This simple phrase captures the laziness of our minds perfectly. It must not be good if it doesn't fit our framework or is difficult to understand.

Our sense of what is "normal" can inhibit us from understand-ing another person's sense of normal. Such lenses hide from our view our underlying assumptions about what we consider to be good and right. If we do not critically analyze how we acquired the knowledge and lenses we have, we will lose out on the opportuni-ties to learn from others and see what we don't see.

We all have had different paths to gathering knowledge, rooted in differences of language, religion, values, geography, climate, family structure and history, and much more. How my Pacific Islander ancestors gathered, processed, and shared knowl-edge differs greatly from my neighbor's Scottish ancestors or another neighbor's Mexican ancestors. How we know what we know or deem *good*, *right*, and *normal* is viewed through a very limited lens. Don't get me wrong, the lens has value, but it is limited. To step outside of ourselves with greater humanity, we need to acknowledge that limitation and recognize that our lenses are developed through the collection of exposure and experience, or what some refer to as *social and cultural capital*.

> Our sense of what is "normal" can inhibit us from understanding another person's sense of normal.

Our view of the world is impacted by the collection of our expe-riences—or our cultural capital. *Cultural*—referring to our unique identities and experiences. And *Capital*—in reference to the assets, knowledge, and skills we have or develop to navigate life. Coined by French sociologist Pierre Bourdieu, cultural capital is the social strata and power dynamics in society influenced by various assets stemming from unique cultural experiences, networks, histories, and environments.[1] In other words, some people have more access to resources and opportunities than others because of various forms of cultural capital like language, networks, education, access to tools and instruments, emotional intelligence, and more. Since Bourdieu, other scholars have challenged his particular categories of cultural capital and have introduced other forms of assets, but the point is similar. Based on a variety of factors in our lives, we each have varying levels of exposure and access to certain benefits or opportunities.

Let's go back to my baseball example at the beginning of the chapter. To play the game of baseball, you need a field, equipment, someone to teach you the rules of the game, and other people to play with you. Your success in playing the game of baseball depends on your access to these assets and opportunities. Some don't know that you run to first base after you hit the ball. Some don't know that they can enter the on-deck circle to get ready to hit. Others don't have a bat to hit with. And yet others were never invited to or told there was a game going on and where the field was. In the game of life, the rules are more complex than baseball, and we need access to education, tools, mentors, resources, and opportunities for growth.

Our forms of cultural capital become so commonplace for us that we not only assume their normalcy but often also deem them to have some moral correctness. We qualify the things we do as good, right, and normal. And, if someone doesn't do the things we do, we might subconsciously deem their activities to be wrong.

Our ways of knowing are not better or richer than other ways of knowing. We need to understand that there are unwritten rules to be learned in various contexts. The rules for success in higher education differ from those in a new family dynamic. Our increased humanity is found in our ability to be learners and translators. We need to learn the rules that govern different frames of normal and value them, and we need to be better translators to those who are new to our frames. The point is to be more mindful of our mental processes and behaviors in diverse settings.

I have conducted numerous teacher trainings in both K–12 and higher education settings. I invite teachers to consider the elements of their hidden curricula—or the messages they don't realize they communicate to signal how to be successful in their classes. At first, most don't acknowledge that they have a hidden curriculum. I then ask, "What do you value in a student?" or "What makes a great student in your mind?" The responses start to reveal what they favor: Someone who asks lots of questions and participates in class. Someone who hands in their homework on time. Someone who behaves themselves during quiet time. Someone who seeks me out after class to follow up on things. These are not unreasonable expectations of students. That said, for first-generation students (those whose parents didn't graduate from college), some of these practices may not be behaviors they've been exposed to and know the benefits of. This requires a combination of students working to learn and teachers helping to navigate. In order to do so, teachers must learn from and about the students to understand how to best meet their educational needs and teach them how to access resources. We must understand that our navigational habits dictate human behavior according to our cultural capital and mental scripts.

The Scripts We Follow

Early in my career, I had the opportunity to visit many elementary, junior high, and high schools with a few federal programs that were meant to encourage youth from low-income and first-generation backgrounds to go to college. As part of an assignment for my master's program in educational leadership, I interviewed students at a local elementary school with a high percentage of Hispanic students.[2] I interviewed a few dozen students from the third, fourth, and fifth grades about their college aspirations, interests, and how they liked school. Students shared similar lofty goals and dreams, and most said that school was important for reaching their goals. For most of the questions, student responses were consistent across racial/ethnic lines. But the responses to one particular question haunted me.

I asked, "If you became an adult tomorrow and worked at this school, where would you think the school would put you to work?" Notice how this question was phrased. Most White students (90 percent) said they would be made a teacher, a nurse, a teacher's aide, or even the principal. Most Hispanic students (76 percent) said they would be made cafeteria workers or janitors. When asked where they would be placed to work at the school, children as young as eight were already noticing certain scripts about the world in which they lived. After my interviews with the students, I asked for a breakdown of the employees at the school by race/ethnicity and found that there was not one Hispanic teacher (there was one part-time parent liaison) or administrator, and 70 percent of the cafeteria workers and janitors were Hispanic. And yet, nearly 34 percent of the students in the school self-identified as Hispanic.

These data are not insignificant when coupled with my

interview findings. They suggest a strong correlation between a lack of representation of Hispanic educators and Hispanic students' perceptions about what is possible for them as they grow up. In their life script, these young people have noted the types of individuals who have leading roles and those who have supporting roles. If they don't see Hispanic educators, the students subconsciously believe that it's not a possibility for them—even before deciding to pursue that career.

When young people see professionals who look like them or share their identities in positions of leadership, interest, or authority, their brains process a new code of possibility that such opportunities are attainable for them. And the more representation, the greater the possibility. When I became a university vice president, I was the first VP of color in the seventy-six-year history of the institution. I had students and staff members of color message me via social media or email or simply tell me in passing on campus that it meant so much to them to see me in this new position as they now saw it as a possibility for them. I know our president, Astrid Tuminez, experienced similar responses when she became the first female and person of color to be our university's president.

Scripts are developed subtly and powerfully through our observations of the world. Children begin formulating what is good, right, or normal based on their identities—how they have been represented, empowered, or diminished through media, music, politics, and national discourse. These scripts influence our propensity to share thoughts, engage in projects, and contribute to our communities. They influence our confidence levels in navigating the world around us and even affect the opportunities we can access.

Throughout the 1940s and into the early 1950s, doctors Kenneth and Mamie Clark conducted a series of experiments called "the doll tests."[3] These experiments were designed to study the psychological effects of segregation on Black children. In the experiment, the doctors used four dolls: a White boy doll, a White girl doll, a Black boy doll, and a Black girl doll. They asked children ages three to seven to identify the race of the dolls and the dolls they believed to be associated with certain characteristics. Most of the children (both White and Black) preferred the White dolls, associating them with more positive characteristics (nice, kind, smart, happy). They associated the Black dolls with more negative characteristics (angry, mean, stupid, bully). After this study, the Clarks believed that racial segregation had negatively affected the self-esteem and self-worth perceptions of the young Black participants. All the children in the study (White and Black) subscribed to a certain script that permeated society.

Seventy years later, Claude Steele's *Whistling Vivaldi* explained his studies of Black students and how internalizing a certain level of racism about themselves related to academic performance.[4] Steele argued that even the threat of a stereotype has a powerful influence on human behavior. He and his colleague, Steven Spencer, conducted various college-based studies about women and people of color negatively affected by the threat of a stereotype of their cognitive abilities. Women and Black students were given various cognitive tests. The female students who were told that the test was a true measure of their cognitive intelligence performed worse than those who were told there was no evidence that men and women performed differently on such tests. Similarly, Black students performed better on cognitive tests if they were told there was no evidence of cognitive difference based on race. The very weight of the stereotype threat affected how students performed in various tests and other dimensions of schooling.

These and other studies have demonstrated the power of scripts in navigating and making sense of the world around us. Scripts, codes, and schemata affect how and why we view the world the way we do. The more mindful we are about the reasons we have certain lenses, the more we can understand how we engage with the contexts and people around us. Humanity-driven people seek opportunities to analyze their worldviews and engage in reflection exercises that help bring understanding about their uniqueness.

> The more mindful we are about the reasons we have certain lenses, the more we can understand how we engage with the contexts and people around us.

Take Action: Characteristic Map

One of the most effective exercises to help us explore how and why we see the world the way we do is called the *Characteristic Map*.[5] The goal is to identify a variety of inputs that have been a part of our lives and map them to how we view the world. In this exercise, we explore three different categories of characteristics or experiences we have had in our lives: ascribed (what you were born into), roles and hats (what your responsibilities have been), and experiences (both positive and negative). You will make a list of characteristics for each of these three categories to begin the mapping exercise. But before you do, let me provide a bit more context for each of the categories.

ASCRIBED CHARACTERISTICS

These are characteristics that you were born into and had no control over. They were ascribed to you at birth. I was born into a family who loved the Los Angeles Lakers; I had no choice in the matter. My father immigrated from the Philippines and worked his way across the US just to make it to the land of Wilt Chamberlain. My favorite childhood memories involve sitting with my father as we watched the Showtime Lakers of the '80s in their classic battles with the Celtics. How does that ascribed characteristic (being a Lakers fan) affect who I am today and why I view the world the way I do? Well, I am still a huge Lakers fan today. I played basketball and still love to play basketball. Any time I meet another Lakers fan, there is an instant connection. I realize that my mood changes depending on whether the Lakers win. It has affected the activities I participate in with my family and the decorations for my office. In short, an influence so small still impacts who I am today.

How much more profound are the ascribed characteristics of first language, religion, and family structure regarding how and why we view the world the way we do today and what we consider morally right and normal? Over time many experience changes in language, religion, or socioeconomic status. However, we cannot deny that those characteristics ascribed to us at birth still affect us today and how we engage with the world.

ROLES AND RESPONSIBILITIES

These are characteristics associated with the responsibilities we've had. The roles I've held and the things I've been responsible for over my lifetime have shifted my lenses significantly. When I became a father in 2004, I remember bringing my son to our small home, placing his car seat on the bed, and staring at him. Why are my lenses as a father so integral to who I am today? Why does it matter? In nearly every decision I make, I cannot take off these lenses through which

I see how such decisions will affect my children. These lenses are evident in even the smallest ways. I cannot go to a park or other public settings and not be concerned when I see a child with no adult nearby. If I see it happen, I immediately start looking around to identify any hint or sign of a parent or guardian who might be connected to the wandering child. I begin to judge every adult within the vicinity and ask why they, too, are not concerned about the parentless kid. The fact that I am physiologically affected by that incident means that I have developed new lenses due to my responsibilities and experiences as a father. As an educator, I often think about how a parent would like their child to be advocated for or cared about, and it affects how I do my work.

EXPERIENCES

You have significant experiences—both positive and negative—that have influenced who you are today. Be honest about experiences that have altered how you view the world. This category is the catchall for any experiences (large or small, positive or negative) that have affected your state of living, mind, emotions, motivation, and trajectory. These experiences have impacted who you trust and don't trust, why you shop where you do, and what you like to do for fun. I love to travel and have had the chance to live in the beautiful country of Colombia. When I learned Spanish in an immersive context (more than just high school lists of Spanish verbs), I began to find new ways of describing the world around me. So what? How did learning a new language affect who I am today and how I view the world? Because my ability to empathize and connect with those who speak Spanish (or must learn a new language) have improved. Because my bilingualism has afforded me work opportunities that would not have been there otherwise. Because I feel a kinship and connection to Colombians and Spanish speakers even though I don't self-identify as Hispanic or Latino. My lenses have shifted because of this experience.

Now that you have a better understanding of the three categories, take out a sheet of paper or open a document on your computer and create a table similar to *Figure 1. Mapping Characteristics Table.* Once you have created the three columns with the appropriate headings, fill in your personal bullet points using the example as a primer to remind you of the distinction of characteristics in each category. Try to fill in at least five bullet points per column.

The next step is to select one bullet point from each list and then write down why that bullet point matters in terms of who you are today, how you navigate your world, and how you view the world. Practice asking yourself a cascading series of the same question: "So what?"

My example: My father was a talented artist but struggled as a businessperson. So what?

1. I gravitated toward art early on but later was nervous about pursuing it as a career. So what?

2. I have been tempted to be entrepreneurial in my career but have valued stability more. So what?

3. When I show up for my students, I tend to advise them with the lens of stability more than risk-taking. So what?

FIGURE 1. MAPPING CHARACTERISTICS TABLE

Ascribed	Roles and Responsibilities	Experiences
• What were you born into? • First language • Geographic location • Family structure • Birth order • Family religion/worldview • Family political leanings • Socioeconomic status • Working parent(s)/ guardian(s) • Gender • Ability/disability	• What roles do you play? • What hats do you wear? • What responsibilities do you have? • What titles do you carry? • Who depends on you?	• What significant experiences have you had that influenced who you are today? • Positive or negative • Person, place, incident • Life-changing/-turning events • Experiences that affected your state of living, state of mind, emotions, motivation, and trajectory
So what?	So what?	So what?

You can see that this line of questioning can keep going, and we begin to realize how much our life experiences show up in our lives more than we fully understand.

This exercise is highly beneficial when done individually, but it can become even more meaningful and rewarding when conducted with others who are open to being vulnerable. There is a power in having to articulate to someone else how life experiences have affected the person you are today.

The Characteristic Map is just one of many lens-check tools to analyze your views of the world more deliberately and how they got there. The key is to be intentional and take the time to improve personal lens-checks. We don't ever fully finish looking inward. Because we are ever evolving and our lenses constantly shift, we need to check in regularly in more deliberate and introspective ways. How and why we know something is as important as what we know. The more we can understand the origins of our thoughts and actions, the better we can understand how to engage with others more effectively.

CHAPTER SUMMARY

- We need to become better learners about how we know what we know. Like baseball or cricket, our lived experiences cause us to understand and value things differently.

- Recognizing that our sense of normal is developed through our experiences and exposure to the world is important. Many things we learn about what constitutes valuable knowledge are the things we are exposed to in both conscious and hidden ways.

- It is important to recognize that we know things because of our opportunities for exposure and engagement. Depending on our life circumstances, those opportunities are on a spectrum, from limited to abundant. The greater our access to opportunities, the more likely we are to learn the written and unwritten rules about navigating life.

- Access to opportunities makes a difference in our social and cultural capital development.

- We subconsciously follow scripts based on whether or not we see people like us in a variety of settings.

- Intentional reflection and self-analysis are important components to gaining a greater understanding of our worldview, our scripts, and our lenses.

CHAPTER 3

Filipino Elvis and Left-Handers: Check Your Lenses Regularly

"We don't see things as they are; we see things as we are."

—ANAÏS NIN

FOR MUCH OF MY CHILDHOOD, I shared a room with my sister. We had a modest room, with beds on opposite sides that doubled as boats on the ocean of our blue, shag carpet. Our father tucked us into bed each night and told us stories of his adventures growing up in the Philippines. In addition to making us laugh with jokes and impressions, he played his guitar and sang to us—not just any lullaby songs, though. He sang Elvis songs. And, I kid you not, he sounded exactly like the King. If there was ever a record of Elvis playing, we actually thought Dad was singing. My father was, in fact, an Elvis impersonator and performed up until his seventy-ninth birthday, shortly before he passed away in 2020. Not only did Dad sing to us each night, he would kiss us on the forehead, tell us he loved us, turn out the lights, and leave the room.

My mom left for work early in the morning, and Dad took us to school. At the time, I thought that every one of my classmates had the same experiences I did. They showed up to school wearing similar clothes. Some were more engaged in class than others, but for the most part, I saw at least one of their parents at the same events my parents attended. Didn't everyone have a parent tuck them into bed every night with stories, Elvis songs, and kisses on the forehead? Didn't every one of my classmates have a full dinner the night before school and a hearty breakfast in the morning? Didn't everyone have their parents drop them off at school and pick them up afterward?

As I grew older, I recognized disparities in the lived experiences of my friends. I observed what was happening in many homes. Kids of all ages were not waiting for a parent or guardian to tuck them into bed. Rather, their single parent worked late, so they put themselves and their younger siblings to bed. Or they hoped their parent or guardian did not come home in a drunken rage followed by spousal or child abuse. Many went to bed with their stomachs rumbling because they didn't have enough to eat but also didn't want to complain because they knew they couldn't afford more. Some students had to take two or three forms of transportation, starting early in the morning, to get to school. They couldn't concentrate on the lesson because they were hungry and cold from a lack of breakfast or warm clothing.

I was fortunate, or privileged, as a child to have the situation I did. I don't believe I'm a bad person because my father tucked me into bed at night. I just didn't have the stresses that others had, and I didn't know it. My children also love bedtime stories, and they don't have to expend any emotional or psychological energy wondering when their parents are coming home, whether they will get something to eat, how they will get to school, or what they will wear that will keep them warm. They do have stresses in life, but they are fortunate not to have to spend energy worrying about things other kids do. Here is the important part—if my wife and I don't talk with them about it, they don't know what they don't know.

Left-Handers

In addition to impersonating Elvis, my father was a fine artist (oil painter) and an architect. He was also left-handed. He was the only left-hander in my family. Between 10 and 12 percent of the world's population is left-handed. For any left-handers reading this, think about activities, experiences, or objects you have encountered in your life primarily designed for right-handers. What comes to mind? Look at the following list and see if any of the items or experiences are things you've struggled with at some point in your life.

• Scissors	• Number pad on the keyboard on the right side
• Zipper flaps on jackets and pants	• Purchasing sporting equipment
• Swiping credit cards on the right side of the machine	• Eating at a restaurant and choosing a seat
• Car cup holders	• The armrest on the individual desks at schools
• Guitars and other instruments	• Tape measure is upside down
• Vegetable peelers	• Three-ring binders and other notebooks
• Camera button	• Can openers

What would you add to the list?

Left-handers have had to learn to live in a right-handed world, and while they've adapted to many things, they still encounter frustrations. Some have even had an authority figure in their life (parent or teacher) attempt to teach them to do things with their right hand so they could have an easier life. Some have even been punished in grade school or boarding schools for using their left hands. If you're right-handed, the next question is for you: How often have you had to process or think about your right-handedness? If your response is consistent with the hundreds of groups I have spoken to, then not many of you have thought about it (unless you injured your right hand and had to use your left hand for an extended period). Right-handers have rarely, if ever, had to think about how they might navigate the world around them. They have simply assumed they can do things as right-handers because they have rarely experienced life where they couldn't.

Humor me with a quick experiment. Find the nearest pen, pencil, or marker, and hold it in your right hand as if you're about to write. If there are words on the pen, can you read them? Now switch hands and place the pen in your left hand. Can you still read it? It's probably upside down. I have yet to find a writing utensil with words on the side that can be read in the left hand. Profound? No. Earth shattering? Not really. But think about it for a moment.

Writing utensils are made with the assumption that right-handers will be using them. It's a smart business decision, as the makers of pens know that roughly 90 percent of potential customers are right-hand dominant. Right-handers are the majority; therefore, we make things that fit into our sense of normal for the majority. And it becomes accepted as something that left-handers just deal with. Again, not a big deal when compared to other injustices in life. But the point is the same. Right-handers are not bad people for being right-handed; no one says they are. The invitation is simply for right-handers to recognize that their sense of normal (as members of a majority) is not everyone's experience. The more cognizant we are of our privileges (great and small), the more we can build bridges of understanding.

The *P* Word: Yes, You Have It, and So Do I

Privilege is one of the most polarizing concepts in the world today. I know the word might not sit well with you, but hear me out. I define privilege as a set of default benefits that come to those who either self-identify with a majority group or who don't have to spend emotional or psychological energy wondering how they will navigate life with their identities or circumstances. And there are parts of our identities that may be privileged and other parts that are not. For example, someone might be in the majority linguistically but in the minority regarding their religion. Another person may be in the racial majority but may not have had anyone in their family go to college. When we are in the majority, we often don't recognize the struggles others might face. Checking our Inner Lens in meaningful and deeply introspective ways is critical when deliberately analyzing one's privileges and how they affect one's worldview. If we don't, we lose opportunities to develop empathy for others who may not be in the majority, thus hindering our ability to show up with greater humanity.

> When we are in the majority, we often don't recognize the struggles others might face because their identities and unique needs have not been considered in the development of societal goods, services, and experiences.

The concept of privilege has been treated in research, social media, and conversations with varying levels of accuracy and animosity on all sides. Why? Because in most cases, conversations about privilege usually end up in a watering down of the topic itself or an all-out verbal battle about oppressed and empowered identities and experiences. I'd like to offer a different approach to privilege and invite you to consider the ownership of your privilege as a key to developing the Inner Lens of humanity.

I don't find it stifling to acknowledge my privileges, nor do I stop engagement because of an overwhelming sense of guilt for the benefits and advantages I have had as part of a majority that others have not. What do we have to lose by admitting that, in various aspects of our lives, we experience a benefit that others don't?

Let's explore a bit more about right-handed privilege. This is definitely on the watered-down side of the privilege spectrum. That said, it is helpful for two reasons. First, it addresses a part of our identity that has never felt threatened or that we don't affix to the core of who we are. Better stated, we don't care if someone accuses us of having right-handed privilege because there are no big social questions and debates about right- and left-handedness. Second, we can at least see how it might be possible for one group to have to spend emotional and psychological time and energy thinking about how to navigate certain situations. In contrast, others don't have to at all. If it is within the realm of possibility, then why is it such a stretch for us to acknowledge other forms of privilege or other situations where majority and minority groups experience life differently? Let's consider another example.

When my wife, Michele, was seventeen years old, she was involved in a car accident driving from northeastern Arizona to Utah. As the van tipped on its side and skidded to a stop, her arm went under the van and was severed inches above her elbow. After a series of miracles, including quick thinking to create a tourniquet from a fellow passenger, a passerby with a cell phone (this is 1996 when cell phones were not common), and being life-flighted to a hospital, Michele began her road to recovery. She decided against having a prosthetic arm and began the next chapter of her life with one arm.

I won't go into full details of her story as that is for her to tell in her book one day. But, the point of sharing a brief portion of it here is yet another example of hidden privileges that we don't think about. I have the luxury of not having to wonder how I am going to do a task with my two arms and two hands. For most of my life, I didn't think about my ability-based privilege. Again, no one has ever called me a bad person because I have both my arms and hands. And yet, through my relationship with Michele, I have developed new lenses of understanding that she does not share the same privilege. On a daily basis Michele must spend mental, emotional, and physical energy figuring out how to navigate this world with one arm and one hand. By owning my ability privilege, I am developing empathy for those who don't have it and can show up for them with more humanity as I learn of their lived experiences.

Capital *P* and Lowercase *p*

Over the years, I have had various students and colleagues ask me about situational privilege vs. ongoing (or systemic) privilege, or as I like to refer to them, lowercase *p* and capital *P*. Some have suggested that, within the privilege conversation, a distinction should be made between the macro-privilege issues (capital *P*) and the micro-privilege issues (lowercase *p*). In making this distinction, I propose a differentiation in the application.

The lowercase *privilege* is what I refer to as situational, temporary, and benign. This category includes individuals who traditionally might be in the majority but find themselves in the minority in certain situations and, therefore, may not see any benefits to one of their specific identities. These moments are usually temporary and are affixed to specific situations, moments, and places. The lowercase *p* also refers to examples like right-handedness, which has low social costs.

Privilege with a capital *P*, on the other hand, is systemic and focuses on the ongoing societal navigation of institutions, systems, and norms. For example, holidays and traditions in the United States follow a Christian faith base. Despite this, there are still moments where someone identifying as Christian—as I do—may have situations where they are in the religious minority. We may feel that Christian privilege does not exist in such moments because we must be extra mindful of our faith in that moment and space. We might feel uncomfortable because our Christian identity is not safe. The discomfort usually comes because we haven't had meaningful engagement with other religious, ideological, or faith groups. Therefore, one might feel their religious identity threatened. But here is where we then shift to the capital *P*. Once that situation is over, we step back into a national or even local culture where we passively accept the celebration of Christian-related holidays (Christmas and Easter) on a large scale and in a way that is not the same for other faith groups.

I have selected a sampling of privileges for those who might be in a majority identity. The list was compiled from a variety of resources and written from a US historical perspective of those who have been in the majority or those who have historically held power. As you read these, I invite you to consider four things:

- First, if you find yourself in the majority (in any of the statements), it is easy to get defensive and dismiss the statements as false for your situation or life. The focus of these lists is on the capital *P* privilege, or privilege that has been historical, systemic, and pervasive. Remember that this is not about you personally, but rather about identities that have historically had more benefits and power than others.

- Second, you might be tempted to argue that some of these privileges have changed in our modern day and are no longer an issue. While this argument may hold some truth in pockets for some groups, the statements selected still reflect a different experience for those in the majority instead of those in the minority.

- Third, remember that this is the chapter on lens-checking and developing stronger approaches to being more humanity-driven, so we need to reflect on how and why it is important to recognize such privileges in our lives and what we can do about them.

- Fourth, the statements are written from a variety of *Capital P* identities, including racial, gender, religious/spiritual, sexual orientation, ability, and linguistic.

AS A PERSON WHO SELF-IDENTIFIES WITH A MAJORITY IDENTITY OR AN IDENTITY THAT HAS TYPICALLY HELD POWER . . .

1. When discussions about our national heritage or civilization arise, the accomplishments of people of my identity are consistently highlighted.

2. I can be sure that classroom and educational materials provided to my children will acknowledge and include positive representations of their identity. It is likely that my children will have teachers who share my child's identity.

3. I can do well in a challenging situation without being called a credit to my identity and am never asked to speak for all the people of my identity group.

4. I can be confident that if I ask to talk to "the person in charge," I will face someone of my identity.

5. I can assume that in the course of my day-to-day activities, services are accessible to me and communication can be conducted in my primary language.

6. As a male, my masculinity will not be questioned if I have children but do not provide primary care. And if I pursue a career, no one will think I'm selfish for not staying home with my children.

7. I can expect to have time off work to celebrate my religious holidays, and music and television programs about my religion's holidays are readily accessible.

8. I do not have to fear that if my family or friends find out about my sexual orientation, there will be economic, emotional, physical, or psychological consequences.

Now for some honest self-reflection. As you read through the statements, did you get defensive, or were you tempted to explain something away with a "yeah, but . . ."? Did you nod your head in agreement with certain points? Did you get a confused look when you read other statements? I share these examples to invite all to consider experiences we may not have deeply thought about before, especially if we identify with the majority. Again, these statements are not meant to divide us but rather to help us reflect on the experiences of other humans in ways that we haven't previously. This reflection sharpens our Inner Lens and enhances our sensitivity for the humanity of others.

I remember the first time I read statements like these. My initial feelings included a mixture of guilt, shame, anger, defensiveness, and a desire to change some of these individual and systemic dynamics. The more I reflected and analyzed my lived experiences (as a Christian, heterosexual, English-speaking, able-bodied, male citizen of color), the more I realized that the statements held truth. This process has led to countless moments of catching myself in privileged assumptions and realizing that I need continuous development of empathy and advocacy for others.

> Our Inner Lens development is limited if we do not honestly recognize our privileges.

Our Inner Lens development is limited if we do not honestly recognize our privileges. To become more humanity-driven, we must practice the ability to see things as others might see them. And we must be willing to check our own lenses regarding sensitivity to the experiences of others.

Lens-Checking: A Room of Mirrors

When I was three years old, I received nunchucks with Bruce Lee's face on them, and I had myself a new hero. He was everything a young, Asian boy wanted to be—a kung fu master and a movie star. In what is widely recognized as his most famous movie, *Enter the Dragon*, Bruce Lee was engaged in an epic fight with the crime lord Han. During the battle, Lee chases Han into a room with mirrors in every direction. In this room, Lee is disoriented but can also see in every direction and every angle of himself.

Have you ever been in a room with multiple mirrors (fitting rooms, carnivals, and even some elevators)? In these rooms, I am fascinated by the angles of my head and body that I rarely see. I glance in different directions to take in new perspectives. The views are interesting and strange, almost like an out-of-body experience. On one occasion, I remember an angle that showed the hair on the crown of my head thinning. This was the first time I realized that I was starting to lose hair, and it freaked me out a little. I remember telling my wife about my hair discovery, and she simply responded, "Yeah, but it's not bad." I was like, "Huh?! You knew, and you didn't say anything?" Michele didn't feel the need to say anything because she assumed I knew.

I have thought about a room of mirrors frequently in my work on self-awareness and cultural competence. Most of us have not put in the time or attention, nor have we had the awareness, skills, and tools, to adequately assess ourselves in a 360-degree fashion. It is hard to see something if we don't know how to look for it. And it is hard to question ourselves when we have spent our lifetime developing and justifying a certain paradigm or way of viewing the world. If unchecked, however, we will miss more important things than thinning hair: we will miss opportunities for understanding and the development of meaningful relationships. I invite you to consider the value of placing yourself in a metaphorical room of mirrors and be intentional about seeing things you've never even known to look for.

Numerous people have asked me if one can develop greater self-awareness, self-understanding, and self-monitoring skills. They ask these questions because they know people who have had countless trainings and exposure, after which there was no noticeable change in how they interacted with others or responded to differences. Lens development depends on an individual's desire and disposition to develop new lenses. They have to care enough about the value of diverse perspectives to even begin to shift their lenses. But what about those who have no desire to change at all? Those who are set in their ways and perspectives? Perhaps these efforts (and this book) are not for them. The goal of this book was never to move the staunch percentage of the population filled with hatred toward difference. This book is for much of the population who, I believe, are open to learning and continuing the conversation. Nevertheless, we can be more deliberate in checking our lenses and reframing our thinking.

In the introduction of this book, I refer to three key concepts that humans long for: stability, connection, and purpose. To arrive at any sense of these, we must first analyze what makes us unique as humans. I don't mean the things that distinguish us from animals, insects, or other life-forms; I mean, *What makes each of us unique as a human?* Our capacity to find stability, connection, and purpose is linked to an awareness of who we are and the unique things we can offer to this world and others. If the goal is to develop lenses of humanity, we must focus our energy and attention on our current lenses and worldviews. The analysis, or lens-check, must not be a one-time exercise, nor should it be a shallow interest inventory. It requires our ongoing honesty, vulnerability, and courage to see how and why our beliefs about other humans are the way they are. It is difficult to help others find safety, relevance, and connection if we don't understand why they matter to us.

It is difficult for us to begin improving our attitudes toward people with diverse perspectives, narratives, and identities if we do not understand our own—and worse if we are unwilling to learn. To be fair, critical self-analysis is not a natural practice. For most humans, the brain functions to help navigate the world around us for maximum safety, comfort, and efficiency. While not necessarily bad, we need to become increasingly aware of our subconscious thought processes as much as the ones we are conscious of. In short, the development of the Inner Lens depends on our willingness to check it often.

CHAPTER SUMMARY

- Privilege is the benefit of not having to spend any emotional, psychological, or physical energy navigating a situation or community with your identity(ies).

- We all have privilege in some ways and lack privilege in others. That said, there are differences between the capital *P* (systemic, pervasive, societal) privilege and lowercase *p* (situational, temporary, and benign) privilege.

- Rather than get defensive about the concept of privilege, let us own what we have and reflect on what we can learn from others about how they are experiencing the world.

- Engaging in regular lens-checking enables us to examine the filters through which we perceive the world, uncover our biases and subconscious assumptions, and gain a deeper understanding of how our experiences and identities shape our perspectives. It encourages us to challenge our preconceptions and cultivate empathy toward others.

PART 2

The Context Lens

Humanity-driven people study and engage with diversity of history, thought, and perspective

Context Lens Snapshot

As humanity-driven people, we recognize the importance of context in our interpretation of everything around us. We become more cognizant of how our mind has interpreted stories in our lives and how they have shaped how we navigate the world. We recognize that the stories we have heard or been exposed to are incomplete and require our engagement with different voices and people. We value new and diverse stories as opportunities for learning and growth, as they provide greater context and understanding—even if initially uncomfortable. We deliberately take actions to educate ourselves and engage with others to develop informed and holistic perspectives of diverse people and communities.

Why a Context Lens?

Context matters. It is critical to our understanding of one another. This lens extends the Inner Lens as we continue to look inward. Rather than focusing on developing our thoughts and perspectives, we expand our analysis through greater exposure to diverse contexts.

We move from looking in the mirror to a 360-degree, panoramic view of the world to understand and situate diverse human experiences. Such a lens informs how we interpret and respond to diverse individuals and communities, thus providing opportunities for meaningful human connections

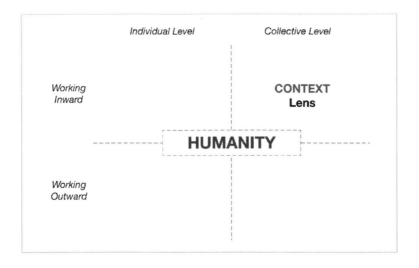

Lenses of Humanity Framework: Context Lens Focus

CHAPTER 4

Comic Books and Graffiti: Analyze the Stories You Believe and Why

"Stories are a communal currency of humanity."

—TAHIR SHAH

MY FIRST JOB WAS AT A BASEBALL CARD SHOP in Canoga Park called Who's on First? In addition to sports cards, we sold Magic: The Gathering cards, rented laser disc videos and video games, and, most importantly for me, sold comic books. It was during this time that my love of comic books as a medium for storytelling was born. I developed my love for drawing from my father. He told us many stories of his childhood in the Philippines, drawing comic books for his friends to rent and read. I always loved looking at comic book art, but I didn't get into the stories until I officially started collecting in 1991. At the time, I thought the stories were incredible: full of drama, real-world issues, and relatable characters . . . or so I thought.

The '90s in comic book history is known as the era of speculation, artist empowerment, and way too many bells and whistles. In other words, it was an era that focused on the gimmicks and allure of the cover art and not so much the storylines. Marvel and DC were responding to a new company, Image Comics, formed by seven hotshot artists who were changing the landscape of the comic book world. These artists (including Todd McFarlane, Jim Lee, Rob Liefeld, Erik Larsen, Marc Silvestri, Jim Valentino, and Filipino artist Whilce Portacio) focused on dynamic new characters, covers, and costumes that appealed to the visual senses. But most lacked the sustainability of strong stories.

Years later, as I began to collect comic books once again, I returned to these same stories of the early '90s. And I laughed . . . but mostly at myself. I didn't blame the artists or companies who were producing such material. I realized that my lenses at that time were different, and what I perceived to be quality comic storylines was not the case years later.

Throughout our lives, we attach value and emotion to our experiences. As we recount such memories, the stories we tell ourselves are constantly changing. They were interpreted through our lenses at a specific time and in a certain context. How often have you visited a place of great importance from your youth only to be underwhelmed by the same place through the lenses of an adult?

A couple of years ago, my family visited Disneyland in Anaheim, and as we approached the Magic Kingdom castle, my oldest son said, with an unimpressed tone, "Wow . . . the castle used to be so much bigger." His mind, at seventeen years old and nearly six feet tall, was trying to remember the story that his mind as a five-foot ten-year-old told him. His story was truth to him because of his lived experience until his perspectives and the story changed.

As a professor of future teachers, I am fascinated by the disconnect between what my students think their teaching experience will be like and what they face in their first year. Their image of a teacher inspiring, motivating, and helping young people in the magical classroom setting often does not match their first semester of student teaching.

We evolve in our understanding of the world and how we want to navigate it. By improving our contextual lenses, we get better at setting incidents, exchanges, and interactions in context for our increased understanding. This elevation in perspective changes our behavior, and our abilities to connect across differences are enhanced. By improving our awareness of historical, cultural, linguistic, geographic, and political dynamics, we are better equipped to develop the two outwardly focused lenses of humanity regarding working with others (Empathy and Community).

Storytelling as reality framing is both powerful and dangerous. No matter where the stories come from—school textbooks, media—and how closely the story hits home—from international religious strife to neighborhood feuds—we, as humans, are heavily influenced by them and the connected emotions more than we realize. And to strengthen our Context Lens, we need to examine the stories we believe.

Learning and Unlearning Stories

We choose the stories we tell ourselves. Do any of these sound familiar? If our child makes a choice that society doesn't agree with or accept, the story we tell ourselves is that the behavior needs fixing and we might be bad parents. If we ever fail a test, the story we tell ourselves is that we are stupid. If we achieve a difficult goal, we tell ourselves that we can do hard things. If I get picked last for a team, my story is that nobody likes me. If we offer an idea at work that our supervisor does not implement, we believe we are not valued. If we exercise for a week but don't see results, the story is that it's not worth it.

Each of these stories we choose adds cards to our mental boxes. As we learned through the Inner Lens, the volume and intensity of experiences captured on those cards influence our behavior. If we're not careful, cognizant, and deliberate about our understanding of these cards, we begin to subconsciously live our lives in ways that confirm the stories in our minds—thus leading to a perpetual cycle of story confirmation about ourselves.

This process happens with others as well. Indeed, it is dangerous to gather stories based on experiences with others without fully understanding the context of that setting, timing, and what the other person brings to that exchange. Context is everything. The more we know about something, the greater our potential to understand it. And the more we know about someone, the greater our potential to understand them.

Context is everything. The more we know about something, the greater our potential to understand it.

When we meet someone for the first time, we observe certain things about them and start piecing together a mental puzzle about how to navigate this new person. The more we get to know someone, the more we learn about their context. As we learn about someone's interests, hobbies, language, fears, dreams, and history, we increase our understanding of their behavior. Their actions and words have more meaning because we know more about where they are coming from.

In addition to developing our Inner Lens and looking inward

more critically, we must take inventory of the stories surrounding us. Look beyond the initial information and seek to gather more—especially when learning about other people. Our ability to make meaningful, humanity-driven connections with other individuals is contingent upon developing our Context Lens. It is difficult enough for us to fully understand how and why we react to certain situations the way we do; imagine how difficult it is for us to understand how someone else might interpret the policies, practices, and situations around them without any contextual understanding of their lenses. Synapses are strengthened through frequency and intensity. The more frequent an experience, the more the brain codes it as a real story. The more intense the situation (good and bad), the more emotion is tied to the story, making it real in another way. We trust what we see repeated and what we feel.

Stories have been used for generations to: capture history, explain origins, entertain, teach lessons, make connections, and evoke emotions. Organizations spend millions of dollars to influence customers' stories about products or experiences. Every cultural community has its way of sharing stories in written, oral, or other formats (ceremony, performance, etc.). But what if exposure to only one story is your window to the world? Chimamanda Ngozi Adichie offered a powerful insight with her 2009 TED Talk, "Danger of a Single Story."[1] She proposes that our lack of exposure to diverse stories and more context creates a limited single story in our minds about other people and other places. With Chimamanda's caution about the single story, let's revisit the library of the mind.

The volume and nature of the cards we collect about a person or identity group shape our story about such individuals. Remember, stories are connected to emotions. The cards of most significance in our mental catalog boxes are those tied to powerful emotions (positive or negative). For example, if someone hears about immigrants but does not have a meaningful relationship or connection with someone who is an immigrant, the cards in their mental box (labeled *immigrants*) will be tied to an emotion of fear due to the media and headlines regarding immigrants. If that same individual gains more exposure to immigrants, the emotions tied to that mental box can shift, depending on the nature of the exposure or interaction. If a positive set of interactions leads to a positive relationship or friendship, that experiential emotion can outweigh the initial fear developed from the casual consumption of media. The more we get to know people, the more nuanced the context, and the more we combat the single story of who they represent.

Our biases about people who identify differently than we do stems from our limited exposure to different perspectives and relationships. Undoubtedly, there are individuals who prefer a lack of exposure to diversity for themselves and their children to maintain a certain way of thinking or believing. These individuals maintain narrowed lenses that can lead to prejudice. This is the story these individuals might tell themselves: *If my children and I are exposed to diversity, our ways of living, knowing, and behaving might be corrupted.* Can you see how this is the opposite of developing humanity-based lenses? Ironically, if we feel judged based on some aspect of our identities, we immediately respond with, "Don't judge me . . . you don't even know me." We are critical of external judgment because we believe others have not done their homework and therefore have a limited or wrong story about us. The stories we are exposed to, live by, and tell ourselves will always be limited until we can value the stories and perspectives of different people.

The Authors of Reality

Winston Churchill famously said, "History is written by the victors," as well as "History will be kind to me for I intend to write it." Napoleon Bonaparte said, "What is history, but a fable agreed upon?" According to *Business Recorder*, "Any attempt to uncover past events and thence to formulate an intelligible account of it is almost impossible without the adulteration of personal view of things, people, places, and events."[2] Mark Twain offered, "The very ink with which all history is written is merely fluid prejudice."

We cannot escape our connection to history as told through the lenses of people society has deemed to be historical experts and authorities. If we know that two different people can experience the same event through different lenses, we know that their accounts of such events will also differ (in subtle and significant ways). Then, depending on our lenses (developed through our experiences), we will attach different meanings and interpretations to both accounts, and we follow with a judgment about such accounts. The problem is that we rarely receive or value two or more accounts of the same event or set of events. This is because storytelling, or history accounting, has been tied to those in power, those in the majority, and those who stand to benefit by sharing only one side of the story.

Stories follow a cycle of power as stories beget stories: The stories about the bombing of Pearl Harbor, the bombing of Hiroshima and Nagasaki, and the internment of Japanese Americans were repeatedly told in certain ways in the United States. In contrast, different stories were regularly told in Japan. Both storytelling efforts were part of the desire to evoke emotion or solidify the story in our minds and hearts because of the emotional connection. This is propaganda at its core—broad messaging that focuses on evoking emotion tied to a message about a certain issue or population. These stories impacted political campaigns, curriculum in schools, and military engagement.

Those in power can position themselves—and by extension, their identities—as the authorities on historical truth. They frame their lives as those of heroes, victims, or courageous humans. What have been the prevailing identities in power throughout history? Primarily those whose identities have been in the majority. I am not criticizing those who share majority identities. Rather, I argue that these identities have been the primary authors of the prevailing stories of society, and they have been incomplete.

If we are to increase our understanding of others, we must recognize the context of how the majority story has framed an accepted reality for so many. That accepted reality begins to justify people's prejudice, fears, and xenophobia if they can frame certain populations as the "other," or people who are not understood well and therefore feared. Our sense of what is "normal" is influenced by exposure to difference. The more our interactions with similar identities and worldviews, the more likely we are to solidify a certain model in our minds of what a "normal" person should look, think, talk, and behave like. Anyone outside that norm can threaten the comfort that exists within the norm. The stories we tell ourselves about what is normal in society deeply impact our willingness to step into new, immersive experiences with people vastly different from us. And this is the danger to humanity of the single story. The more individuals are threatened by the other, the more they revert to the comfort of their echo chambers. Bridge-building and mutual understanding (key elements of humanity) are harder to achieve when this retreat occurs.

The need for intentional engagement with diverse stories is

nowhere more evident than in the classroom. When considering our authors of reality, we need to be honest with ourselves about how much our schooling experience taught us to critically think, weigh diverse perspectives, and engage in debate. Although many teaching practices have improved in this regard, there are still far too many classrooms where memorization and passive knowledge consumption are the norm.

The Classroom and Curriculum

As mentioned in chapter 1, the institution of education is one of the most influential laboratories for developing our sense of place, identity, and self-worth. The classroom is also significant regarding our collective understanding of truth and history. We can each remember something we learned in elementary school that we unlearned at some point later in life. In my case, it was along the history of Native Americans set within a curriculum in California that promoted California's history. A localized approach to the study of history is common in most, if not all, countries due to the promotion of some sense of nationalism or country pride. In the US, states will often include units and curricula that focus on that state's history in addition to US history. It is not until the sixth grade that US students typically explore world geography and global history. However, due to limited classroom time, there is only an introductory and shallow view of civilizations and incidents deemed globally noteworthy.

My schooling experience provided a very shallow treatment of Native American history. My memories are filled with discussions of Indians during Thanksgiving, with half the class dressed as cowboys and the other half as Indians. Mention was made of a few Native American tribes in California during one unit covering California history, but that was it. Most discussions of Native Americans suggested that Indians were a part of history and only a part of history; in other words, they were irrelevant today and didn't carry on any sacred traditions, ceremonies, or even languages. These schooling experiences coupled with my lack of exposure to Native American people meant I had a single story about American Indians, as if they were one people. I wish I could say that similar things don't happen today in schools, but I cannot.

Later in my life, through courses, friendships, immersive experiences, and ultimately my relationship with my wife, Michele, the story about Native Americans changed for me. But why was the story so hard to undo for many years? History is not only written by the victors but also by the literate or those with literary skills and devices to capture history. Most indigenous cultures worldwide shared stories orally for centuries, as many languages were not developed in written format. As languages began to develop on paper, it took time for individuals to learn to capture the history of such cultures and peoples. The historians became those who had

- readily accessible writing tools;

- training in literary works to capture stories and histories in a written format;

- writing in a language already developed in written format for centuries; and

- ways to produce, preserve, replicate, and disseminate the written account.

The history that influenced school curricula was created, if not by the victors of wars, by those who had the resources, education, tools, and commonality of their language in written format. In short, those who influenced our textbooks have primarily had the privilege of their circumstances to do so. While many changes are underway to infuse diverse approaches, perspectives, and histories into school curricula (with varying levels of commitment by schools, school districts, or states), it is important to understand how foundational school curriculum is in terms of our general exposure to the outside world. At such a young age, we formulate stories (or scripts, from chapter 2) that can dramatically impact our behavior and desire to engage with differences.

Humanizing Unheard Stories and Flipping Scripts

In the fall of 2009, I was asked to join a local gang-prevention task force. One of the areas of concern for the city was the increased volume of graffiti. As I sat with the task force in meetings, I was struck by the language used to describe the graffiti artists—*taggers*, *vandals*, and *troublemakers*. I raised my hand and commented that I believed these young artists were quite talented. I talked about the motivation for young people to put up public art without permission as an effort to be seen. Many young people are not acknowledged in their schools as adding value. The messages they have received most of their lives and the stories perpetuated about them suggest that no one expects them to succeed in school. The societal script for them was negative. I asked if I might have an opportunity to see if we could get these young artists to college. The task force agreed, and we set up an initial meeting at our university museum of art.

In February of 2010, we invited eighteen young artists—many of whom had a juvenile record due to graffiti—to attend a college info session focused on street art. Fourteen showed up. We provided pizza, and I brought my sketchbooks. The artists brought theirs as well. We sat in a circle in our university museum and talked. Each artist introduced themselves, stating where they were from, how long they had been writing (graffiti), and why they were engaged in it. This was a two-hour conversation, filled with personal stories and raw conversations about negative interactions with the law. To close the evening, I talked about our proposal for the program. I told them we wanted their artwork displayed in our museum of art, and we wanted them to lead a community-wide conversation about the power of street art. We discussed some of the elements of the program, including weekly art sessions, college prep sessions, mentoring, and donations from art shops of canvases and spray paint. We had their attention. More importantly, we had begun a journey that would challenge the scripts and stories the artists had about themselves as well as the stories others had about them.

Eight young men committed to the program one month after our initial conversation. Over the next few months, we helped them finish their accelerated coursework materials to receive their high school diplomas or prepare for the GED. We worked with them on developing artist statements, and they taught each other graffiti techniques. They read a book for the first time with the program. Then, in the fall of 2010, they took an art museum curation class and a painting class to help them develop their museum pieces around the theme of "Hidden Voices." We collectively chose this as the exhibit theme as an entry point for a conversation with the community about why the artists engaged in such work. Our dialogues revealed a common thread among the artists. They didn't feel a sense of connection at school and never spoke up in class but felt liberated and valued when they were engaged in street art. They even filmed their documentary titled *Why Do I Write?* and showed it at the exhibit.

Two months before the targeted exhibit opening night, the artists met with the museum curator and mapped out the needed preparation for the exhibit space. The artists then worked to finalize their canvas pieces and their artistic statements. They made flyers to invite people to the opening night. We gave them white ties, black button-down shirts, and exhibitor badges so that everyone would know who the artists were on opening night. We had worked with these young artists for nearly a year to help flip a script built up over their lifetimes.

Finally, on January 18, 2011, we gathered the eight artists and their families in a banquet room across the hall from the museum. I told the family members to be proud of their son's, grandson's, and brother's work. We talked about all that went into having their work hung in an official museum of art and our desire to help the community reframe how they think about these young men as contributors to our community.

At 7 p.m., we walked the artists and their families to the museum, where people were already admiring the work that hung throughout the three galleries. Some were engaging in an interactive graffiti wall. Some answered questions on a magnet board about whether graffiti is art. Others were looking at books about graffiti and street art worldwide. Some put on headphones in the mini theater to watch the documentary. But most patrons were looking at the large canvases that adorned the walls. Each artist stood next to his piece and greeted guests by explaining the story behind his art. The entire night was filled with constant chatter and mingling. I welcomed gang-prevention task force members who showed up with their families (and not in police uniform) to take in the show. About ten university administrators attended, and at about 8 p.m., we started a mini program including words from our associate dean of the School of the Arts, the museum curator, and two artists. We then had a surprise visit from our university president, who applauded the boys and gave all eight admission letters to the university and scholarships to two of the artists to the honors program.

Throughout the night, 540 people attended the exhibit, and over the six weeks of its run, 2,500 people visited. For some who attended, the scripts in their minds had been flipped. One of the most touching stories of the night included one of the artists and his younger brother. I first noticed Nestor's little brother by his side at the dinner. Then, throughout the evening, every time I saw Nestor, I saw his little brother at his hip, with a big smile. Later that night, Nestor shared with our group that having his little brother shadow him the whole night meant a lot to him because he knew that for many years, his parents had been telling his younger brother, "I don't want you to be like Nestor." And that night, having his parents and younger brother so proud of their college-bound artist meant everything to him. Script flipped.

There is a power in our ability to share or create space for new stories—not necessarily in an aggressive or opposing way but sometimes in a way that invites people to consider new perspectives, angles, and lenses.

There is a power in our ability to share or create space for new stories—not necessarily in an aggressive or opposing way but sometimes in a way that invites people to consider new perspectives, angles, and lenses. The gang-prevention task force had a certain story established in their minds about graffiti artists. It was a story that was accepted by most in the department. After experiencing the exhibit, one of the officers said, "I can never look at a graffiti artist the same way again." Story learned. Context gathered. Understanding improved.

The more exposure we have to new and diverse stories, the more we value the humanity of people, and the greater our ability to situate experiences and conversations in their appropriate contexts. We have regular opportunities to invite more humanizing, unheard stories into our lives to help shift our contextual lenses. In our communities, social circles, and organizations, who don't we know, and who haven't we heard from? Are there identity groups with negatively associated cards in our mental boxes, and what are we willing to do to humanize their stories?

CHAPTER SUMMARY

- The development of a contextual lens is influenced by the stories we believe or have embedded as part of our narrative.

- The stories we hear and the stories we tell affect our behavior and our interpretation of the context of any given scenario or interaction.

- A lack of exposure to different stories and perspectives leads us to believe a single story about a population or identity group. The more exposure we have to diverse stories, the less likely we are to develop a "single story" or prejudice about the other or someone different from us.

- The majority story has been created throughout history by those in power or who had the resources, tools, and formal training to capture stories in written format.

- Schools are influential in shaping our understanding of specific stories. We learn about the world around us from very scripted lenses of nationalism, localism, or simply the majority experience.

- We have opportunities to create spaces and places for diverse stories to be told, heard, and valued—all with the effort of gathering context and increasing understanding.

CHAPTER 5

Leonard Bernstein and the Devil's Interval: Reframe Dissonance as Healthy

"What if we saw differences in cultures, in moral choices, and in belief as reasons to engage people instead of excuses to disengage and quickly exit?"

—HOLLY SPRINK

LEONARD BERNSTEIN GREW UP TAKING PIANO lessons at the Garrison and Boston Latin Schools. Later, he attended Harvard University and the Curtis Institute of Music in Philadelphia to study piano, conducting, and orchestration with some of the world's finest composers. One of Bernstein's most recognized works is the score to the famed Broadway musical *West Side Story*. This legendary 1961 story of forbidden love between Tony and Maria is set in Manhattan, where two rival gangs clash in cross-cultural battles for respect and territory. Inspired by Shakespeare's

Romeo and Juliet, *West Side Story* became an instant classic for its contemporary adaptation, choreography, and music.

When composing the score for *West Side Story*, Bernstein made a bold choice to build the music around an unsettling interval known as "The Devil's Interval." It is a tritone that is so dissonant it earned the nickname *diabolus in musica* or "the devil in music." And Bernstein didn't just use it once—he used it throughout the score. The consistent use of dissonance created tension at key moments of the musical. Occasionally, the tritone would be resolved, lowering storyline tension and achieving musical satisfaction. Bernstein recognized that one of the most powerful uses of music to tell stories was an intentional interruption to the harmony that had listeners sit up, lean in, listen more closely, and seek resolution. The Devil's Interval, like all dissonance, requires people to be more aware, cognizant, and invested in understanding.

Throughout our lives, we encounter differences that can be jarring. Many of these experiences elicit anger, confusion, and embarrassment. After all, they disrupt our life's harmony and rhythm. They disrupt comfort zones, predictability, and the management of our expectations. What, then, can we do to be prepared for such encounters with difference, so we don't feel disoriented, disrupted, or lost? More importantly, how do we develop an open disposition to see such encounters as opportunities for growth? We must be deliberate and open about the frequency and depth of exposure to difference, and we should seek out and reframe such dissonance as healthy opportunities for learning.

Healthy Dissonance:
Purposeful Engagement with Difference

We don't like to be uncomfortable. We don't like to be wrong. And we don't like to be told that we are ignorant or that our worldview is misguided. Humans default to comfort, efficiency, and pleasure for survival. Much like our desire to hear a beautiful harmony, we want some predictability and consistency in our lives. However, a humanity-driven approach to life requires us to deliberately opt in to moments of dissonance or experiences that we expect will be jarring, yet helpful to our development. In the words of Neale Walsch, "Life begins at the edge of our comfort zone." Like Bernstein's score, the dissonance might initially be disruptive and uncomfortable. Still, the more we listen and intentionally stay with the musical, the more the dissonance becomes a rich opportunity for understanding, appreciation, and growth.

When I consult with organizations, I often ask how the organization might provide explicit opportunities for its students, employees, or community members to meaningfully engage with differences. Working with one university, we explored the actions that could be taken to welcome a culture of healthy and diverse exchanges. As we planned, we wanted some situations to be purposefully diverse in the viewpoints represented and the thoughts offered. We also wanted to model how university students and employees might engage in civil and respectful debate. During one of the sessions, someone said they were experiencing some dissonance but liked it. When asked to elaborate, the participant said that she was tempted to retreat when the conversation started getting heated but asked herself, "What can I learn from this exchange?" She shared that the moment she switched her perspective from fear to learning, the uncomfortable situation became an opportunity for growth. At a conference, I heard a speaker say, "Our goal is to become comfortable with the uncomfortable." I understand what they were trying to communicate, but it's not that simple. I think our goal is to bravely engage with difference as a healthy exercise, even if uncomfortable.

We could all use a bit more healthy dissonance in our lives. I define *healthy dissonance* as purposeful engagement with something that is going to cause you to pause, wake up, or feel uncomfortable for a moment but that ultimately allows you to learn, grow, and develop. In short, healthy dissonance is engagement with difference that leads to growth. Through this view, our desire for resolution is not simply to return to harmony or comfort but to heighten understanding and clarity. It is the invitation to opt in when you want to opt out. The irony is that the more one opts in to the dissonance, the more one gets used to navigating new and potentially challenging situations. Their exposure to the dissonance no longer rattles them, and they know how to bring the conversation or engagement to a healthy place. The goal is not consensus. The goal is not to return to comfort but move forward in understanding. The goal is growth through deliberate engagement with difference. Frank A. Clark famously said, "We find comfort among those who agree with us—growth among those who don't."

> **The goal is not consensus. The goal is not to return to comfort but move forward in understanding. The goal is growth through deliberate engagement with difference.**

But we also have to be careful. You do not need to opt in to potentially dangerous or even abusive situations just to jar you from comfort. Each of us must understand our limits regarding energy and the type of self-care needed so that engagement with difference leads to learning and growth, not depression and isolation. Notice I am not advocating adding more challenges or dissonance to our lives just for fun. My invitation to lean in to opportunities for healthy dissonance is related to engagement with different perspectives. You need to be the judge of whether or not the engagement is healthy.

Another potential danger of deliberate dissonance is how we facilitate cross-cultural learning. Some diversity trainings like to use shock tactics to make participants feel uncomfortable. I have lost count of the number of individuals I have met who expressed some frustration with a "diversity" or "inclusion" training they received where they felt attacked, berated, and blamed for various ills of society. To those individuals, I often ask, "Why did you feel that way? What about the way the material was presented caused you to have that reaction?" They usually point to the presenter's style or approach.

As I've observed fellow consultants and trainers, I have noticed three general approaches to conducting such trainings: (1) shame people for their implicit role in one or more of society's historical inequities or problems, (2) point out the societal problem and ask people to consider what they have done to resolve or add to it, or (3) softly introduce the problem but have no dialogue or introspection about the individuals' contributions to it. The first scenario misses the "healthy" portion of healthy dissonance, and the last approach misses the actual dissonant moment. In other words, we all have limitations on how we want to engage with difference and discomfort. If the environment for engagement is generally safe, we are more likely to lean in. If not, we retreat, fight, or throw up a wall. But again, too much focus on safety and comfort can lead to no dissonance, no resistance, and therefore limited growth.

We see similar results if we extend these approaches to physical fitness training. We will likely be deterred from returning if the training is overwhelming, uncomfortable, and painful. If the training doesn't push us at all and there is no resistance in weights or challenges in stretching, we are left comfortable but with no progress. In both cases, we have missed opportunities for growth. The difference between healthy and unhealthy dissonance is the intentionality and openness of both parties to seek understanding and learning.

Many individuals proclaim that they are great with change. Still, most don't love change, which usually means a step outside our comfort zones, routines, and carefully curated expectations. By the way, it is called a *comfort zone* for a reason. Famed scholar, speaker, and vulnerability expert Brené Brown shared, "We need to lean into the discomfort" to experience growth. And yes, doing so is a vulnerable exercise because we are unsure where it will lead. As individuals seeking to develop humanity-driven lenses, we must lean in to and engage with people's diverse perspectives. The goal is not to simply be comfortable with the uncomfortable. The goal is to develop an overall disposition to engage with difference because we value it— even if it might be painful sometimes. This helps us have a deeper understanding of diverse people.

Dissonance and Fatigue

Is there a limit to the benefits of dissonance—even healthy dissonance? If you follow the logic that dissonance leads to growth, then wouldn't you want to have it all the time? The answer is no. We each have our human limits, and we are entitled to some level of comfort at times in our lives. We want to be understood, appreciated, and valued, which usually occurs with people who are like us or truly understand and value us. While we can learn much from a healthy debate, very few want to live in a constant state of it. Why? Because it can get tiring, and it might even lead to disengagement. So while we want to get better at engaging in healthy dissonance, let us also practice a level of self-care so we are ready for the next engagement.

We must also recognize that, as we develop new lenses, what may have once made us uncomfortable will no longer do so. In that case, becoming more comfortable with what used to be uncomfortable is possible. In other words, the frequency and nature of our engagement with difference can lead to its normalization in our lives. For example, religious and spiritual identities are not topics that are often comfortable to discuss in the professional setting. Yet, they are an important part of people's identities. The more I engaged in interreligious, interfaith, and cross-worldview work, the more comfortable I became in talking about religious and ideological differences, nuances, and tensions. Once such things are normalized, they become part of our everyday rhythm and comfort zones. It is not surprising, then, that each generation seems more open to difference. This shift is primarily attributable to the sheer exposure to difference and access to diverse stories, perspectives, and experiences.

Are we the only ones who are tired? No. Any time we face resistance in anything we do, it is more tiring. How much more significant is it, then, for an individual who feels resistance in their lives wherever they turn? This resistance could come from ongoing tensions regarding racial, gender, or religious minority identities. The pressure of such circumstances can lead to the proverbial emotional balloon being inflated to the point of explosion. Then, when an explosion occurs, we pay attention to the immediacy of the loud noise and the mess made. We don't pay attention to the small moments of inflating that balloon little by little that led to the bursting of limits.

Those of us in privileged circumstances (myself included) can determine what type of dissonance we can opt in to. We have the privilege of tuning out certain uncomfortable truths about the inequities in our society. If we wanted to, we could ignore some of the dissonance that other individuals and communities feel.

Some people feel dissonance daily simply because society still has not dignified or humanized their identity/identities. This unhealthy dissonance has been a condition of marginalized communities throughout history. I'm not suggesting that people only fall into the privileged or

> Some people feel dissonance daily simply because society still has not dignified or humanized their identity/identities.

not privileged. As mentioned in chapter 3, there is a spectrum of privilege. However, I don't want to miss the point that as we seek to develop our contextual lens, we must all step outside of our variations of privilege to learn about and understand new contexts and perspectives, even if such contexts might be uncomfortable.

Developing a Healthy Disposition toward Difference

So how do we meaningfully engage with difference? First, the literature on cultural competence teaches us that it starts with one's attitude or disposition toward difference. Our dispositions toward difference are reflected in our genuine willingness to learn from that difference. In teacher preparation programs, we assess whether students have the right disposition to teach. In social work, we determine if someone has a disposition to do no harm. In nursing, we ascertain if a nurse has a strong bedside manner. These and many other examples highlight that humanity-driven practices are more relational than transactional. The disposition to teach and champion all students differs from the techniques one might know for classroom management or math methodologies. For pre-service teachers, a candidate's disposition reflects their attitude toward the overall teaching enterprise. We want to know that when problems arise, the teacher can be a creative problem solver and find a way to help their students be successful.

Studies conducted at UCLA found that bedside manner is one of the most crucial parts of a patient's recovery, as it helps build trust in the patient and leads to better care after the patient has left the hospital.[1] Other curricular changes in medical schools include a focus on empathy, caring communication, real-life experience, humor, and technological connections. These are all efforts to recognize patients' humanity and encourage doctors and nurses not to become disconnected health-care providers. The focus is on a relationship between a human who is a medical expert and another human who is a patient.

Once we have a healthy disposition toward difference, it becomes much more natural for us to engage and learn from it. Remember the card catalog boxes and the difference between those with the most cards with positive associations of Middle Eastern men and those without? The difference was the level of exposure and meaningful engagement.

CHAPTER SUMMARY

- Like Bernstein's Devil's Interval, we need dissonant moments to lean in, pay attention to, and work toward resolution. Dissonance, or exposure to difference, can be healthy and can lead to growth.

- The Context Lens is developed the more we are willing to courageously lean in to discomfort and embrace a sense of healthy dissonance in our lives.

- Some dissonance can be so jarring that we avoid anything that could replicate that experience. We must intentionally step into healthy dissonance and provide healthy dissonant moments for others.

- Not all people have the privilege of stepping in and out of dissonant moments. Due to their identities, they might live in a regular state of discomfort or dissonance. We need to recognize this.

- The development of a strong Context Lens requires the development of a healthy disposition toward difference.

CHAPTER 6

Building Bridges and Filling Wells: Engage Meaningfully with Difference

"The more one has engaged in a particular pattern
of thought, the more difficult it becomes to
override these habitual patterns."

—BRYANT McGILL

BRIDGES ARE ONLY NEEDED WHEN THERE is a chasm between two land masses. To build a bridge to another land mass, we must know that the other land mass even exists. So it is with difference. To build bridges of understanding between different people, we must first recognize that there is a difference in how people experience and view the world and that such experiences and worldviews are valuable, contextual, and worth knowing. We cannot build bridges to land masses we don't know exist. And we cannot make meaningful connections with diverse individuals without valuing and understanding their contexts, identities, and narratives.

To improve your Context Lens, you must first be deliberate in your exposure to difference. While there are many ways to increase understanding of diverse humans, there are three basic layers to developing such lenses: (1) exposure, (2) education, and (3) engagement. Each of these three levels can lead to the deepest level—that of meaningful relationships. But while we're still focused on developing the Context Lens, let's unpack these three layers.

Layer 1—Exposure

How do we get better at knowing what we don't know? Some individuals may be perfectly content to stay in a social or ideological bubble, without any desire to build bridges with different people. However, I assume such individuals will probably not pick up this book. By reading this book, I assume you want to increase and improve your exposure to different people, stories, and perspectives.

Lens development takes work. Our Context Lenses rely on our commitment to doing the labor and work; opting in to dissonant experiences and uncomfortable encounters is easier said than done. Often, we would rather not spend energy getting involved in the mental and emotional tension of engaging difference. Yet, there are ways we can lessen the intensity of the tension. One aspect of developing a strong Context Lens is recognizing that you have much to learn about the world around you. The more you learn, the greater your understanding of the surrounding factors that influence how and why others view the world and behave the way they do. Remember Adichie's "Danger of a Single Story." A lack of exposure to difference causes us to be myopic in our understanding and interpretation of people who are different from us. M.J. Prest's words come to mind: "I thought it peculiar how one new experience can alter your perspective on places you've known your whole life."

There is power in mere exposure to difference. Think about your own lived experiences and pick a moment of exposure to anything new. Whether from new flavors, new languages, or new perspectives, we broaden our mind's library from exposure to new things. Think about conversations you have been in where your thoughts and ideas were challenged. Did you continue to think about those conversations afterward? Yes, you did. But why? Because there is a desire in our minds to find resolution and solidify our beliefs and views or to reconcile new information with old. Exposure to difference also reduces our shock factor when confronted with new data. We begin to embrace new experiences because we appreciate the growth that comes from a broadening of possibilities.

I recently engaged in a meaty conversation about spirituality, sexual orientation, gender identity, parenting, education, and a host of other topics. The group consisted of diverse individuals with a variety of identities (age, gender, religion, sexual orientation, profession, and more). After nearly two hours of unstructured conversation, we expressed gratitude to one another for the vulnerability, trust, and openness. As we left, we talked about how

And by talking with one another so sincerely and openly, we brought that exposure to each other—thus enhancing learning for everyone.

meaningful the conversation was. And days afterward, we shared that things were said that we each pondered deeply. It was apparent that during the conversation we each had varying levels of exposure to different aspects of the conversation. And by talking with one another so sincerely and openly, we brought that exposure to each other—thus enhancing learning for everyone.

Layer 2—Education

While *education* can be broadly defined, the focus is on formal and informal learning opportunities that engage different perspectives, voices, and histories. It is difficult to draw up on an empty well when we need to make meaningful connections with others but never took the time to become educated about them. There are various ways to fill our learning wells if we hope to have something to draw from in future encounters with difference. The education opportunities are vast. An incomplete list includes formal and informal courses, reading new texts, listening to podcasts, watching TED Talks, and more. Remember that we always have opportunities to learn and opt in to learning experiences without enrolling in school or paying tuition. This is where we demonstrate our willingness to do the work of broadening our understanding.

If we are serious about learning, we will set aside time to do our work, fill the well, and not expect others to always take the time to teach us about what we don't know. There are countless resources at our disposal, but we are often not intentional enough to prioritize this type of learning.

One of the most profound ways we can become educated about human difference is by diversifying the stories and voices we invite into our lives. I have found that learning comes from contextualizing new information and asking ourselves, *So what? How do I feel about that new information?* As teachers, we often give our students timed tests, which has led to an educational tradition that puts too much weight on memorization and test scores. In my classes, I have been able to assess student learning more often through dialogue and reflective writing than through timed tests. While certain subject areas necessitate memorizing and recalling information—particularly in disciplines like medicine—deeper learning occurs when students apply the content to real-world experiences. The goal is to engage in meaningful learning experiences. Many aspects of formal education today could benefit from a refresh to ensure their relevance to students.

Consider your own schooling experience, from kindergarten to college. What were the learning experiences that were most meaningful to you? Learning opportunities should push our minds to consider and reconsider. How do we become more critical consumers of available information? How do we truly become 360-degree thinkers? We do so through exposure to various lenses and perspectives and being intentional about learning.

Layer 3—Engagement

When we have an encounter with diversity, what do we do? Do we engage or disengage? Through engagement (usually through dialogue), we find understanding and growth. Disengagement leads to entrenched echo chambers, assumptions of the other, and limited learning. Engagement doesn't need to lead to agreement to be valuable. Increased understanding is a worthy pursuit.

Engagement mitigates the dangers of echo chambers. Each election year, the country is divided into political camps that minimize the complexity of issues and the true range of thoughts to two prevailing ideologies. The 2020 election was no different. According to a Pew Research Center survey of US adults between September 30 and October 5, 2020, the country was dramatically polarized.[1] Eighty-nine percent of Trump supporters said that Biden's election to the presidency would harm the US. Only 4 percent of Trump supporters said they would not be concerned if Biden were elected. Ninety percent of Biden supporters said that Trump's reelection would lead to lasting harm to the US, and only 1 percent of Biden supporters stated they would not be concerned if Trump were reelected.

The danger here is not in the mere difference of ideologies or worldviews. Rather, it lies in the limited binary of two political lenses or camps that position one another as the enemy. During election years, even those who recognize the complexity and nuance of issues can lose track of the opportunities for bridge-building dialogue, human connection, and deeper understanding. The groupthink dynamic of political parties reduces human interaction to an "us vs. them" mentality when there actually might be some agreement on many issues. The way we approach political discourse often does not invite thoughtful commentary but rather incites emotional verbal attacks that cause people to throw up walls, limiting growth for both people. We need to be wary of political extremes in any direction. The extreme political views assume a zero-sum game where it is "all or nothing." Humanity work doesn't operate that way. A lens of humanity starts by assuming that through engagement, understanding can take place along various lines, even if there continues to be disagreement on specific issues.

Social media outlets like X (formerly Twitter), Facebook, and Instagram have exacerbated these echo chambers. These platforms have now set people up for lobbing strong opinions at one another without the nuance of dialogue and authentic engagement. We can scream at one another through the computer without ever having to understand the person's context, background, and experiences that led them to the views they have. If our brains are influenced by repetition of small chunks of information, and we have an emotional response to that information, our brains process it as a truth or a possibility. Some platforms limit the context we could provide to sound bites or limited characters. This forces us to become marketers relying more on tagline and bumper sticker messages than complex, context-driven commentary. In short, we are in an era where we don't have to have meaningful engagement with difference. We believe that someone is the enemy and therefore offers no value. It is here that our individual and collective humanity suffers. We need to combat our lazy brain by being more intentional about what we engage with. I wonder what would change in our society if we individually and collectively moved from being politically-driven to more humanity-driven.

Engagement with difference requires a recognition of the value of difference. Engagement reflects an investment of time, energy, and resources. When engaging with someone or having a new experience, we demonstrate openness to learning and a commitment to understanding. Engagement opportunities can surely be found in educational opportunities and vice versa. However, the distinction I am making between these two levels of exposure is the next step of intentional interaction with people. At the education layer, one could simply receive information from their computer, from books, or by listening to podcasts. These learning opportunities can be effective as we become enriched with new knowledge and perspectives. The engagement layer involves an exchange with someone or an investment in an experience.

> When engaging with someone or having a new experience, we demonstrate openness to learning and commitment to understanding.

Lens development is an ongoing process that requires intentional effort and engagement. Through exposure, education, and engagement, we strengthen our Context Lens and deepen our understanding of diverse perspectives. Education fills our learning well with diverse voices and perspectives, while engagement invites us to actively interact and invest in meaningful experiences. Engagement allows us to see the world through new eyes, navigating language, cultural contexts, and diverse teaching sources. By building bridges of understanding, we transcend our own perspectives and embrace the value of difference. By filling our wells with exposure to new ideas through education and engagement with diverse individuals, we have greater context to draw upon for connection. Together, let us seek new experiences, embrace discomfort, and engage with difference to contribute to a more inclusive, compassionate, and humanity-driven world.

CHAPTER SUMMARY

- In order for us to build bridges with people, we must first validate their existence as different and valuable to learn from.

- There are three layers of bridge-building and context-gathering that we need to act on: (1) exposure, (2) education, and (3) engagement.

- Level 1—Exposure to difference creates opportunity for bridge-building. The greater our exposure to diversity of thought, experience, and perspective, the greater our ability to build meaningful connections with people.

- Level 2—Education includes formal and informal forms of learning new perspectives. The key is to build time in our calendars for learning and filling the well. The more intentional we are about prioritizing our own learning, the more natural it will be for us to understand and make connections with others.

- Level 3—Engagement requires a deliberate exchange with an individual, community, or organization to learn from them.

PART 3

The Empathy Lens

Humanity-driven people learn from and improve empathy for diverse individuals

Empathy Lens Snapshot

Humanity-driven people seek to make meaningful connections with others—especially those with different backgrounds, beliefs, and perspectives. We show up in our interpersonal communication, believing we always have something to learn, and intend to engage in a mutually beneficial educational exchange. We actively seek to understand people to empathize with them. We do our best to validate people by seeing them, hearing them, and using humanizing words and language. We support and advocate for people without historically equitable opportunities for dignified living and empowered voices. We value each person's humanity in how we show up for them.

Why an Empathy Lens?

We desire to be connected to other humans and understood by them. Much of our world's turmoil and conflict is rooted in some inability to work interpersonally, communicate meaningfully, and develop empathy. The core of so much tension, controversy, and war is our inability to communicate with, empathize with, and understand one another. We need to improve our interpersonal relationships, engagements, and communication. The Empathy Lens is the first of two outward-facing lenses. This lens focuses on seeing the humanity within people and ways to meaningfully connect with them.

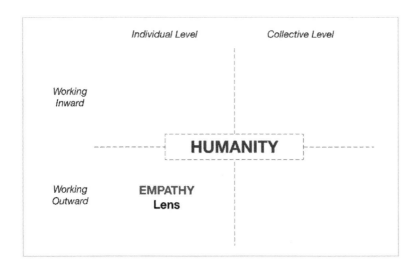

Lenses of Humanity Framework: Empathy Lens Focus

CHAPTER 7

"You Are Not There to Teach": Cultivate Cultural Humility

"Humility, gentleness, and helpfulness go so much further and open doors you cannot imagine."

—ANN TRAN

ONE OF MY MOST REWARDING EXPERIENCES as an educator was with a group of students who opted to do seven weeks of their student teaching on the Navajo Nation, in northeastern Arizona. As part of our curriculum, we provided culturally immersive teaching experiences for students in diverse communities, both worldwide and in the US, to enhance their cultural competencies. I worked with Navajo educators in northeastern Arizona for over a year to develop this teaching experience.

As my students prepared for their immersive teaching experience within the Navajo Nation, we talked extensively about their roles as teachers and learners. Yes, they would be teaching in the K–8 classrooms on the Navajo Nation, but they needed to develop the lenses to learn from the students, parents, teachers, and school staff if they wanted to grow from the experience. In fact, for all our culturally immersive teaching experiences in the School of Education (China, Peru, Tonga, New Zealand, Switzerland, Chile, and the Navajo Nation), a key component of our curriculum was discussing with the students the importance of developing greater cultural humility throughout their experiences. We told the students, "Yes, you are student teachers, but you are not there to teach. You are there to learn."

In their required pre-trip class, students were given readings, assignments, and discussions about indigenous history, Navajo culture, indigenous teaching methods, and cultural immersion. A rotation of Navajo educators and guests joined and taught every class. In addition to the readings and other aspects of the curriculum, the students were asked to begin meaningful engagement. They were invited to attend the university powwow, interview someone who self-identified as Navajo, and share a meal and conversation with a Navajo family.

I then led the students to Ganado, Arizona, where they lived with host families for seven weeks and taught in elementary and middle schools. During the seven weeks, my students had to work through cultural differences, waves of cultural adaptation, differences in school and classroom approaches, and lifestyle changes. They learned how to make tortillas, prepare mutton, and much more. More importantly, they felt the rhythm of the land, learned the cadence of the people, and developed a stronger understanding of how and why Navajo students approached schooling the way they did.

Far too often, we approach new situations and want to impose our sense of what is "right," but we are unfamiliar with the larger context of relationships, timing, location, and overall cultural dynamics. To strengthen our Empathy Lens, we need to view all people as potential teachers from whom we can learn. We don't have to agree, but we can learn from everyone's experiences. Much of the animosity and strife today is an extension of a lack of cultural humility. This world needs more, not less, humility if we are to bridge cultural and other divides.

Humility Takes Courage

Cultural humility is a strength. *Humility* is often associated with being quiet or docile, but this is a misinterpretation of the word. Humility is openness to learning and understanding. So how does one improve cultural humility? Listen more and talk less. Ask questions and learn. Do not be afraid to praise someone else for their insights or experiences: it does not diminish you one bit. The courageous and culturally humble are not afraid to admit mistakes, apologize, and seek to rectify wrongdoings. They understand that interpersonal relationships are strengthened as vulnerability is demonstrated.

Cultural humility invites us to approach difference with a view that other people have strengths (knowledge, skills, stories, abilities) that we can learn from, no matter their background, education level, identity, or language. Cultural humility suggests that we can learn from those we might disagree with or who hold very different perspectives, ideologies, or worldviews. It takes courage to admit that you might be limited in understanding the world and may even be wrong. This is a very difficult thing for us to do. We are naturally inclined to believe that our view of

> **It takes courage to admit that you might be limited in understanding the world and may even be wrong.**

the world is not just correct but also morally right. And such views influence how we treat those who are different from us. Cultural humility invites us to value the knowledge and lived experiences of individuals we may not understand. If the learning leads to us changing our minds about issues because we empathize more with another human. This is not a bad thing.

What happens when you show up with cultural humility, but the other party does not? This situation is bound to occur, highlighting the importance of the courage to show up for others in this way. The natural temptation is to fight back when someone passionately argues with you, matching their negative energy. Do not let them control your energy or how you show up. This is a test of both courage and humility.

Cultural humility does not ask me to defer to someone else's point of view. Rather, the concept reminds me that, no matter the strength of opinions, the other person I am speaking to is a human with a set of life experiences completely different from my own and who probably believes that their perspectives are morally right in the same way I believe mine are.

How we show up to engage with one another says a lot about our fundamental beliefs about the dignity and humanity of others. I have heard people say that they could never treat someone with respect who doesn't respect them. I understand the sheer lens of justice in that life approach. Still, it is a vicious cycle of misinterpretation, lack of communication, assumptions, and judgment. We can be healers of dignity within people. How often have hardened and bitter disputes found resolution or healing by one of the two parties apologizing sincerely and working on learning from the another? Think about the relationships in your own life and the tensions you hold with certain people. I am not suggesting you must go and apologize to everyone. However, I wonder how cultural humility from either party might change how we show up for one another. Our ability to develop the Empathy Lens is affected by our ability to demonstrate cultural humility.

Genuine Inquiry

If we believe we can learn from others, we must improve our ability to ask more meaningful questions. One of the most effective ways to gauge a person's cultural humility is to assess how well they employ genuine inquiry and curiosity in interpersonal relationships. Genuine inquiry is evident when a person asks authentically curious questions to learn from or understand another person. While this may sound intuitive, it takes a bit of intentionality and practice. The next time you are conversing with someone, try to consciously think about whether you are asking authentically curious questions with the intent to learn.

When asking questions, I recommend open-ended ones that allow the other person to more fully articulate a thought or opinion. Questions that will result in a yes or no or quick and finite answers should be reserved for certain surveys. Open-ended questions let the receiver know you are there to listen and learn and want more than a simple answer. Most people love to talk about themselves and their lives—allow them to do so. And remember, the goal of the dialogue is not to reach a consensus but rather to seek understanding. The operative word here is *genuine*. Our questions and inquiries need to reflect an authentic desire to learn. It is easy to tell if someone asks a question from a place of genuine inquiry or goes through the motions of asking questions. Often, people simply listen long enough to speak and be heard.

When it comes to controversial topics, individuals often talk "at" one another. We formulate our thoughts and arguments while the other person is talking—thus not actually listening—and then spout our opinions to ensure we can counter the argument while it is still fresh. Next time you are tempted to do this, pause and ask more questions to learn more context about their perspectives. This allows you to understand more fully what might be at the core of their arguments and opinions.

When someone is in the mode of genuine inquiry, you can tell because they are listening intently and asking follow-up questions. The tone of these conversations tends to be lighter because the overall approach is one of a desire to understand more than to win the debate. People are not on the defensive quite as much, and if both parties are willing to engage in genuine inquiry, they are both authentically open to considering new perspectives, pausing to process, and learning more.

Throughout my career, I have found that questions of genuine inquiry not only invite learning and understanding but also have been powerful tools for de-escalating tense situations. One of the most frequent questions I get in my consulting work is "What do I say if I hear something derogatory, racist, sexist, or discriminatory in some way? I don't want to ignore it, but I have also had bad experiences when I've called people out on it." This is a great question, and I imagine many are not sure what to do in these situations. Here is my general approach to what some call "hot buttons" in a conversation or a moment that has the potential to become a heated exchange.

> Throughout my career, I have found that questions of genuine inquiry not only invite learning and understanding but also have been powerful tools for de-escalating tense situations.

1. I want to know what the goal of a response is. In other words, when you respond to this hot button, what is the goal? Advocacy? Educating the person? Shaming them? Teaching them a lesson? Educating everyone else who is listening? Establishing expectations of what is appropriate and not appropriate? It is important to understand what we are trying to do with our response to gauge how well it achieved that goal.

2. Depending on the goal, the setting, the power dynamics, and the audience (a group vs. just the two of you), there are several ways to respond—each with intended and unintended consequences. We need to be aware of how we received it and how our effort to correct it may lead to walls going up, immediately and in the future.

3. I have found that for most hot button moments, a question or set of questions of genuine inquiry has helped to address the situation, provide clarity, invite more dialogue, and provide space for counter thoughts in a way that drives toward understanding rather than wall-building and grenade-launching.

As an educator in a historically homogeneous area, I encountered this situation repeatedly. In many exchanges I've had with people wherein they have said something incendiary to me or something I passionately disagreed with, I took a breath and asked a series of questions like the following:

- That sounds like a strong opinion; can I ask where that is coming from?

- Is there a reason you feel so strongly about that?

- Are there any experiences you have had that made you feel that way?

- Have you always felt that way?

- You used this word to describe someone; why did you use that word?

- Why did you feel the need to tell me that?

- Do other people you know feel this way?

- What do you suggest would be a solution to that issue?

Questions like these have led to more conversation and more context, which allowed me to learn about their lenses and understand the background of their comments. Then I asked if I might share some perspectives or views that they could consider. If I was authentic with my curiosity about what they had to say, I usually found that individuals were more open to my thoughts if they knew I came from an understanding place. Again, this can't be fake.

Remember, the goal is not simply to win the argument. Have you ever argued with someone about some aspect of life? How often does shouting at one another help? The courage comes in our control and our ability to not let the differing opinion rile us up. The moment we allow that to happen, our view of their humanity gets blurred, and we treat them more as a disconnected enemy. I am not suggesting that a calm approach always yields positive outcomes. In the cases of explicit racism, sexism, and other blatant discrimination, people need to be called out and addressed. However, I return to the goals of the situation and our assessment of how such "calling out" is done. I have rarely seen where fighting fire with fire has resulted in a positive path forward. Yet, on many occasions, I have seen individuals who may have completely opposing views have a productive conversation rooted in a desire to authentically listen and learn, even as they walk away with differing ideologies about the issue.

Reciprocity as Multidirectional Learning

Cultural humility also calls for a commitment to reciprocity or the mutual exchange of benefits, knowledge, and understanding. Reciprocal relationships are multidirectional. Both parties can have a meaningful exchange for growth and learning. However, our ethnocentric brain leans toward a belief that how we learned something or how we view the world is the right way. And as we have learned in previous chapters, our biases about what is good or right show up as cultural pride, not cultural humility. This type of cultural pride hurts our ability to develop mutually beneficial relationships.

Those who have lived, worked, and studied globally and have deep, meaningful relationships with individuals from various countries and communities find they don't need to beat their chests with ethnocentric statements. Through exposure, education, engagement, and immersion, such individuals develop a mindset and disposition that values global and cultural differences. There is no need to declare one nation, community, or culture to be the best, as there is a recognition of the value and assets of various cultures, perspectives, and worldviews. The more we show up with ethnocentric views, the more we limit growth.

There are times when even our efforts in charity take on a singular direction in learning. I grew up in a home where charity was valued, and I think it still holds tremendous value today. My caution is not about charity itself but rather the potential for disconnectedness between the givers and receivers, as if there were clear lines between those who have something to give and those who don't. I fundamentally believe that we all have something to give and something to receive from one another.

Most definitions of *charity* focus on one entity (an individual or organization) helping another entity (individual or groups of people) who is usually perceived as financially impoverished or in need of resources. I believe the premise here to be good. Sharing what one has with another out of a sense of love or compassion is a noble goal and a powerful gesture. So why my caution? I'm not promoting a stop to charity, charitable acts, or teaching the next generation to be charitable. I am simply asking us all to consider that acts in the name of charity can sometimes lead people to subconsciously believe that they are better than other humans. Why? Because much of what we deem to be charitable work is disconnected from the human exchange and thus from the experience of humans learning from one another.

Some believe that there is nobility in anonymous giving, and at some level, I would agree. But I also believe that there is humanity in engagement and reciprocity. I recognize that many who give charitably do so without the expectation of accolades or fanfare. Some shy away from such things and relish the "giving from a distance" approach. Again, while this is admirable, I want us to consider the overall goal of the charitable act. The act is one-directional and transactional—a charitable person gives, and a person in need receives. What would happen if the person who gave were to engage the receiver a bit more, learn about them, understand their strengths, and learn from them? And how much further would the good deed go if the receiver felt empowered to reciprocate in some way?

In my role over fundraising for UVU, I saw countless exchanges of reciprocal giving as donors and students connected. On many occasions, donors and board members told me that they had been the recipients of rich experiences due to their interactions with students. This is why we invite donors to meet with the students who benefit from donated scholarships. It allows everyone to engage and humanizes giving and receiving in both directions.

Humanity seeks to learn. Anonymous charity without engagement and learning misses out on the benefits of relationship. When this happens, multidirectional empowerment and growth are limited. Humans are grateful to receive but find greater joy in the empowerment to give of themselves and be of value. Remember safety, purpose, and connection. Our commitment to reciprocity, mutually beneficial exchanges, and co-learning create much richer opportunities for kindness to move in both directions. True humanity is not in the simple act of giving but in connecting with other humans in a way that dignifies their worth and communicates their value.

We can see the power of reciprocity in family relationships as well. Parents have opportunities to regularly engage with their children and learn from them. I know there have been many opportunities I have missed to connect with my children, truly listen to them, and see their humanity. But in the moments I have been more intentional about seeing them through lenses of humanity, I feel an openness to really learning more about them and from them. Such learning has a way of coming full circle for parents and children later in life.

> **True humanity is not in the simple act of giving but in connecting with other humans in a way that dignifies their worth and communicates their value.**

Humanity is relationship-building that both gives to and receives from another. In this reciprocal approach, we both offer of ourselves and we value what someone else has to offer, thus dignifying them and elevating their humanity.

Take Action: Removing the Wall Exercise

We all have relationships we care about that have been damaged due to poor communication or offensive things that were said. The walls that are created in these relationships can get thicker over time if not intentionally addressed. Using the concepts of cultural humility, genuine inquiry, and reciprocity, here are four steps to remove the wall or prevent that same situation repeating itself.

Step 1: Make a list of three to five individuals in your life who have worldview opinions that are different from yours. Next to each of their names, write the issues or topics you disagree on. Try to be specific instead of using general statements like "all things political."

Step 2: Select one of the individuals on the list who you need to work with to remove the wall from your relationship. Write down everything you know about where their opinion is coming from on a specific topic. Then make a list of questions you'd like to ask them to understand a bit more about why they have such strong opinions.

Step 3: Reach out to the person and schedule a chat. Let them know about the exercise you are embarking on and that you are in a listening and understanding mode. When you meet, proceed to ask the questions you prepared and take note of how the person is responding (what they are saying and how they are saying it). Don't forget follow-up questions of genuine inquiry. Get to the bottom of why they perceive the "wall" was created in the first place.

Step 4: Explain your perceptions of the wall incident and why you have the opinions you do. Continue the exchange in a reciprocal approach as both giver and receiver of information and learning.

In the majority of cases when people I have worked with have employed this approach, they have reported that it led to a strengthening of understanding, a healing of the relationship, and a lowering or removal of the wall.

CHAPTER SUMMARY

- Cultural humility takes courage and requires an honest self-assessment about: (1) the recognition that one's worldview is limited and can therefore be flawed and incomplete and (2) the belief that one can authentically learn from another—especially someone with a dramatically different worldview.

- Genuine inquiry, or the skill to ask open-ended follow-up questions to seek understanding, is a sign of cultural humility and leads to increased understanding and empathy.

- Reciprocity and multidirectional engagement are what humanize and dignify people.

- Removing the walls and barriers in our relationships requires intentionality, cultural humility, genuine inquiry, and reciprocity.

CHAPTER 8

"Just Call Me Susie": Humanize Communication and Dignify People

"I believe freedom begins with naming things.
Humanity is preserved by it."

—EVE ENSLER

WHILE STARTING A NEW SEMESTER OF my Introduction to Public Speaking class, I welcomed my students and had them introduce themselves. One Mongolian student shared her name and said, "But you can just call me Susie." I immediately asked her what her preference was, and she said, "Well, my name is hard to pronounce, so Susie is just easier for everyone." I repeated, "Yes, but what would you prefer to be called." She quickly replied, "It really doesn't matter to me." Sensing that she didn't want to drag this out anymore, I continued with the other class introductions and review of the syllabus.

After class I asked "Susie" if I could chat with her briefly. I apologized to her for putting her on the spot about her name. Then I shared a story about why names mean so much to my family and why the names were chosen for each of my children. I asked her who had given her the name Susie. She talked about having such a difficult time with people mispronouncing her name, and some students even teasing her, so she just chose a more Americanized name to not deal with it anymore. I asked her if her name had any significant meaning. She said she was named after her grandmother, and it was a special name to her, but she had come to resent it because of her US schooling experience. I asked her if she would be willing to teach the class how to pronounce her real name, Soyolmaa (pronounced So-yohl-mah), and if she would be OK with us using it when referring to her. She agreed. I had the whole class come prepared to discuss the origin of their names (first, middle, or last) and why the names were significant to them.

It was one of the best classes I've ever had and actually led to a change in my curriculum for all the courses I taught. We all learned so much about the origins and significance of names and people in their lives who were their namesakes and with whom they had a special bond. When it came time for Soyolmaa to introduce herself, she wrote her name on the board and helped the class pronounce it correctly. It was beautiful and courageous. After class that day, I asked Soyolmaa to always be proud of her name and use it while she was in the US. She agreed and expressed gratitude for the whole experience.

Names, Identity, and the Importance of Naming

Why do names matter so much? Several studies have shown that if students perceive that the teacher knows their name(s), they are more likely to feel included and welcome in a classroom environment, perceive that their teacher cares about them, and have positive learning experiences.[1] Organizational psychologist Joyce E. A. Russell said, "A person's name is the greatest connection to their identity and individuality. Some might say it is the most important word in the world to that person . . . It is a sign of courtesy . . . When someone remembers our name after meeting us, we feel respected and more important."[2] Sociologist Karen Sternheimer said, "Knowing who others are, and others knowing who we are, is the primary building block of social life . . . when we are known and not anonymous, we are more likely to behave in ways that reflect positively on our identities."[3] Author Jennifer Stanchfield said, "Knowing and using each other's names in a respectful way builds trust and positive communication establishing a supportive group environment."[4]

As Michele and I considered names for our children, we felt strongly about making connections with our cultural heritages. We decided that each of our kids would have Hawaiian first names and Navajo middle names. We spent time consulting with family members, thinking about the meaning of each of the names and the messages we wanted our children to have through their names. Throughout their lives, we have talked with them about the meaning of their names and tried to make specific efforts to connect them with their diverse cultures, ancestors, and stories. Kekoa, Ikaika, Iosepa, Ka'imi, Akoni, Keawe, and Anuhea have all had opportunities to teach friends and teachers the pronunciation and meaning of their names. And each time they do so, they solidify a part of their identities.

The history of who gets to name identities is well documented. In many cases, European explorers who colonized new lands and captured their experiences in a written record had the power of naming or giving people certain identities. Later, for political reasons, governments were concerned about identity markers like Native American blood quantum, racial segregation, and Japanese American loyalty. Then, other forms of identity became a part of the political discourse related to inequities (farm workers, voting, gender, sexual orientation, socioeconomic status, English language learners, autism, etc.). Labels and names were used in a derogatory fashion to keep people in socially stratified groups. Later, the same names and labels were co-opted by the groups themselves to reposition them as the owners of the identities. These groups organized, grew in numbers, and were guided by influential activists and advocates who fought for their right to define their own experiences.

Today, each person has myriad intersections of identity with pronouns, titles, preferred names, multiple descriptors, and nuanced terminology. And that is wonderful. With various political parties claiming that the other side is using identity politics, let us be clear about why it matters.

Claiming one's identities is an extension of the discussion on naming. *Naming* refers to one's power and ability to use words that affix meaning to something. Drawing upon our previous discussion about curriculum and the writers of history, winners of wars have been able to name or frame history in a way that favors them. The process of naming and renaming needs to be understood in the larger debate about political correctness.

I do not present lists of words that should be used or avoided in our current day. Socially acceptable language today may not be so tomorrow—and that's the point. Our vigilance around words needs to be high. To become better at humanizing communication, we must remain attuned to the changing dynamics and influences of language, experience, power, and identity on how words are interpreted. Again, is it just a matter of being politically correct? Through the lenses of humanity, no. Our efforts to be more cognizant and sensitive to what people prefer to be called are aligned with our sincere desire to see them and recognize them as unique and valuable humans.

> **Our efforts to be more cognizant and sensitive to what people prefer to be called are aligned with our sincere desire to see them and recognize them as unique and valuable humans.**

One of the most heated debates in the US over the past thirty years has centered on immigration. Strong opinions and complex policies have been presented on various sides of the immigration debate. The two basic camps remain: (1) immigration should be more heavily regulated, limited, and enforced, and (2) laws should change to allow for increased and easier immigration opportunities. The first advocates the rule of law, fear of limited resources, and danger of unchecked foreigners. In contrast, the second promotes the changing of unjust laws, an abundance mentality of resources, and the United States as a country of immigrants. But my intention in sharing this information is not to debate immigration policy. I set this context to analyze the power of words and the danger of dehumanizing words. There are two prevailing terms used to describe the immigrant population who enter the US outside of the sanctioned immigration process or through the designated process but then have their paperwork expire. The political right uses the term *illegal*, while the political left uses the term *undocumented*. Let's unpack this and understand why such words have important distinctions and tones.

The term *illegal* is dehumanizing when referring to people. It is used regularly by those who want to paint certain immigrants as law-breaking and reckless individuals. Many who are US citizens break the law every day, but because of political propaganda, the term *illegal* is never thought to be attached to the majority of people who have broken one law or another (minor or major). The term *illegal* has been primarily affixed to immigrant populations of color. It has created an "us vs. them" mentality—even among other immigrants. Remember the danger of us vs. them when trying to move toward greater humanity. It immediately positions *the other* as an enemy and not worth human dignity. The political left uses the term *undocumented* to highlight that certain immigrants don't have immigration documentation. Each political side has chosen to "name" a population for different reasons.

And this is not the only public debate about how individuals and communities get labeled or named. How do we navigate this issue through humanity-driven lenses? The answer is quite simple: find out how people want to be referred to. Like the situation with Soyolmaa, we can ask people about their preferences. The more we stay in consistent engagement with diverse people, the more quickly we can pivot and become better at humanizing individuals with the names and words that resonate with them. Many have asked, "Haven't we gone too far with this political correctness stuff? We can't say anything anymore without offending someone." With an Empathy Lens of Humanity, I don't see a specific line that has been crossed when trying to name and rename our identities and lived experiences. Rather, I focus on how the other human I am meeting feels about the words they use to describe themselves and their experiences. And it happens to everyone. Something that may not seem significant to one person may be important to another. The way people refer to our ethnicity, sexual orientation, religion, gender, political affiliation, or even geographical location can either resonate with us or set us off, depending on the context and their language.

The Power of Language and Words

Words are powerful. Understanding the power of words matters if we are serious about bringing more humanity into our lives. Most wars, disagreements, and broken relationships begin with a breakdown in communication and the words used to accuse, harm, and misrepresent each other. We can think of specific moments in our lives where words deeply impacted us, for good or bad. Remember our discussion of how our young brains code and process information (chapter 1). As young social scientists, we learn that words have value and can be a source of delight or pain. We have learned that the adage "Sticks and stones may break my bones, but words will never harm me" is untrue. Much of our greatest sources of pain have been because of the words used to criticize, objectify, abuse, and belittle us. And yet, I somehow believe that if you're reading this book, you're not the type who thinks you are too aggressive with words. This is not as simple as setting up a list of bad and good words for us to avoid or use. I think, for the most part, we understand how and why we use certain words the way we do. The argument here is much more subtle but profound: How can we become better curators of the words we use to humanize our interaction with another human?

Our interpersonal relationships influence how we make sense of the world around us. We don't interpret the world in the absence of the human experience. Who we are and how we navigate society is socially constructed. Our sense of identity and place are not developed in a vacuum but in complex relationships. Depending on the relationships in our homes, communities, schools, churches, and businesses, we react in certain ways to different stimuli. And, as we learn in chapter 4, the stories we have internalized about other individuals have influenced our interactions with them. If not interrogated, the stories we believe about others affect our ability to communicate meaningfully with them and can hinder our ability to show up for them in a humanity-led way.

Our words reveal a lot about us. Better said, our word selection reveals much about who we are, what we value, where we stand politically, our exposure to difference, and our limitations in understanding. Our words highlight our education, geography, cultural background, and profession.

As a consultant on cultural competence, multicultural understanding, diversity, and equity, I have worked with hundreds of organizational leaders who are somewhat nervous about engaging in diversity work. Their nervousness often stems from a fear of the words that will be exchanged and their lack of understanding of what the new words mean.

I remember as a young child being frustrated with my parents because they didn't seem to understand what I was trying to say or communicate. As I have grown in age and experience and expanded my vocabulary, I have achieved greater clarity with the words to name my experiences and feelings. Once again, this speaks to the value of exposure, education, and engagement. I don't believe I would have learned Spanish as quickly if I had not intentionally sought to learn it, practiced with native Spanish speakers, and engaged in a context that required my usage of Spanish to navigate my environment. I still remember the first night I dreamed in Spanish. When I awoke, I mentally replayed some of the details. I chuckled to myself that the language was Spanish, even in my mental replay. I also remember trying to explain a Spanish word in English with various descriptions, none of which adequately captured the essence of the Spanish word. My lenses were shifting regarding how I could express myself in the world and my background understanding of how I could communicate better across some cultural difference. Whether it's new language acquisition, reading books, taking classes, or having conversations, we pick up words to help us achieve clarity and communicate our feelings and values.

Take Action: Labels and Meaning

In my classes, this exercise has led to meaningful reflection about names and labels.

- Take out a sheet of paper or open a new document on your computer. Create two columns labeled *negative* and *positive*. In each of the columns, write down or type the words, labels, and/or names you've been given in your life, either under *negative* or *positive*. The same label will have different meanings for different people.

- After spending a few minutes writing down the names and labels, reflect on what you wrote. Or, if you are in a group setting, engage in discussions in pairings of two or three individuals. Each person will then select one label or name from each of the two columns and discuss how such a word has impacted them and influenced how they show up in the world.

The most effective reflections and conversations take place in an environment where vulnerability is modeled, encouraged, and validated. The more exposure we have to understanding why and how people interpret names and labels, the more we are equipped to be sensitive to the power of words when interacting with others.

Body Language, Tone, and Approach

Tone and body language influence how a message is received more than words. Mehrabian and Ferris's landmark study about the determinants of our communication impact on someone found that our body language determines 55 percent of how the message is received, our voice determines 38 percent, and what we say determines 7 percent.[5] We have all experienced moments when we missed what was said because we were already so turned off by the tone and body language.

In response to invitations to improve our approaches and communication tones, I have heard from a few students and colleagues the following excuses regarding the development of new communication skills:

- I am just hardwired that way.

- I grew up in _____, and we just communicate that way.

- People know that's how I am, and they seem to accept it.

- I don't want to be fake. I want to be authentic in my communication.

In response to each of these statements, I ask, "What are your goals with human relationships?" Most humans desire to be heard, understood, appreciated, and valued. The invitation to be more intentional about how our communication is interpreted across differences is not an invitation to be fake or disingenuous. We all have an opportunity and the ability to improve our approach to caring and humanizing communication. Our progress hinges upon our desire to improve and the actions we take to improve.

We need to become more mindful of how our communication styles can align with more humanity-driven interactions with people.

Most of us believe we are great communicators, but we tend to have an overinflated view of our communication effectiveness. In almost every study exploring the difference between a self-assessment and a peer/direct report assessment of communication effectiveness, the individual has a much higher perception of their effectiveness than others in the survey. If we accept these results, then each of us should be a bit wary of our overconfidence in our current communication styles. What does it mean to communicate with more humanity?

Most of us believe we are great communicators, but we tend to have an overinflated view of our communication effectiveness.

We have all experienced situations in which a message has been misinterpreted, misunderstood, or flat-out missed because of the body language, tone, and overall approach to the communication—from one or both parties. If not addressed, such situations escalate and morph into a toxic game of telephone where the main message is co-opted by emotions. Our fight-or-flight systems and mental habits begin to categorize the other as the enemy; and once that happens, we empathize less and dehumanize their existence to feel better about our animosity for them.

I recognize that we are emotional beings, and I do not advocate for a distant and robotic response to emotional communication. The invitation is to look inward and recognize how our approach to interpersonal communication can hinder our ability to learn from, understand, and build connections with diverse individuals.

To be successful in this world, moving forward (if we care about humanity), we must remain vigilant and humble about the changing nature of words, identity markers, names, and tones. The next time you are tempted to aggressively respond to someone because they have a different opinion or worldview than you, remember the concepts of humanizing communication. It is not always easy to approach life in this way. But our growth and understanding of others depends on it.

Humans yearn for connection. Nothing strengthens connections and relationships more than interpersonal communication. We derive value from communication with those around us. Each exchange with another person is like a dolphin's sonar, where signals are sent out. Based on the time it takes for the signal to return, the dolphin can gauge the distance of something. We, similarly, communicate and make mental notes about where we stand. Our place in the world is based on how our communication has been received and returned. Does our body language or tone communicate an openness to learn? Are we cognizant of our eye contact, distractions (phone), and other variables impacting the communication?

A critical part of developing the Empathy Lens in our pursuit of a humanity-driven life is our understanding that one-to-one communication needs to become a greater point of analysis and study for each of us. Meaningful conversations, relationships, and friendships have brought about the most profound changes in the hearts and minds of people.

Humanity-driven individuals spend time and energy working on improving communication skills. Why? Because they recognize the importance of human connection through communication. Improving our interpersonal communication can dramatically affect every aspect of our lives, including our relationships in our homes and with extended family, and in our workplaces, communities, and various personal and professional connections. Critical to developing our Empathy Lens of Humanity is a more deliberate effort to humanize our communication with others.

CHAPTER SUMMARY

- Learn and use names and labels that people prefer for their own identities. Names and how we identify matter to each of us. By respecting how others have named and labeled themselves, we help to dignify their experiences and their humanity.

- One of the components of clear communication is using appropriate words and terminology. Words matter, and our ability to constantly learn new terms and words to build trust and connect better with diverse individuals indicates our humanity. We must expand our vocabulary and choose words that humanize other people.

- Communicate with a tone and approach of respect for the humanity of others. Our body language, voice, and tone all impact the messages we are sending and how they are received. It is difficult to build human connection if people don't want to hear what you have to say because of how you are saying it.

CHAPTER 9

"Your Mom Is Proud of You": Demonstrate Active Empathy

"Empathy is really the opposite of spiritual meanness.
It's the capacity to understand that every war is
both won and lost. And that someone else's pain
is as meaningful as your own."

—BARBARA KINGSOLVER

EARLY ON SATURDAY MORNING, APRIL FOURTH, 2015, my wife woke me and told me my sister had been trying to reach me and wanted me to call her immediately. The moment Noreen answered, I could hear her sobbing, and she quickly explained that our mom was in the Kaiser Permanente Los Angeles Medical Center with bleeding in her brain. The doctor's early diagnosis was that Mom would not last long. She had fallen and hit her head, causing a mini hemorrhage. The doctors encouraged the family to arrive quickly, as they did not know how long she would last. They placed her on a ventilator to keep her heart going, but she showed little to no brain activity. I assured Noreen that I would hop on the next flight to LAX. Michele consoled me for a moment and brought me my laptop. I quickly looked up the next flight, packed a few things, and was on my way to Los Angeles while Michele stayed with our young kids.

I don't remember everything going through my mind, but I was processing deep emotions. On the way to the airport, I called a faculty colleague, Dr. Raquel Cook, and told her the situation. We were about to lead an alternate Spring Break student experience together, but she immediately said, "Go! I'll take care of everything. Go and be with your mom." Raquel did not hesitate to take on the burden of such a complex trip.

On the plane, I didn't want to sit by anyone. I didn't want to talk with anyone. I wanted to hide against the window and perhaps even sleep, hoping to wake up from a bad dream. A woman on crutches sat next to me, and I turned to pretend to be asleep as we took off. About twenty minutes before we landed, I was awakened by the pilot announcing that we were starting our initial descent. I'm not sure if I ever actually fell asleep, but I was dazed and somewhat disoriented. Apparently, it was so evident that my neighbor asked, "Are you OK?"

I looked at her with swollen eyes from crying. Half asleep, I muttered, "I'm fine."

She asked, "Are you going home, or are you visiting someone?"

Caught off guard by the question, I answered, "A little of both. I'm from LA, but I live in Utah now."

She continued with her questions. "So, do you still have family in LA?"

There was a long pause, and then I lost it. I teared up and told her exactly what I understood to be happening with my mother. She turned her body to face me, grabbed a packet of tissues from her purse, and listened to my ramblings. She then asked me a question I was not anticipating: "What do you do for a living?"

I told her I was an educator, "just like my mom."

She smiled and said, "No matter what happens today or tomorrow, I want you to know that as a mother and an educator, I know your mom is proud of you."

Her words were like a warm blanket. She said something so sincere and with such compassion that I felt the depth of her humanity. We talked for the rest of the flight. When it was time for us to say goodbye, she hugged me as I hurried to exit the plane.

That evening, my brother arrived and joined me, my sister, and my father as we each rotated and took our private moment in the room to say goodbye to Mom. When it was my turn to say goodbye, I held her hand and thanked her for everything she had taught me. I became an educator because of her, and I wanted her to know that I would try to carry on her legacy of care for students—especially those who have been underserved in schools. As we removed Mom from life support the next day, we gathered with more family around her bedside. With my dad playing the guitar, we sang songs, including "Aloha 'Oe"—a Hawaiian song with the lyrics "until we meet again." Hours later, as they took Mom away, my sister and I stayed in the hospital room, held each other, and cried.

Layers of Empathy

Countless individuals empathized with our family on three levels: cognitive (they could understand what we were going through); emotional (they could feel what we were going through); and compassionate (they wanted to comfort us). The combination of their understanding and feeling led to acts of service, big and small, to help us heal and alleviate our pain. Some knew what we felt, as they had lost a parent not too long before. Others knew about our family dynamics and that our mom was the glue that kept us together. Some, like my airplane companion, understood the bond between mother and child and said exactly what I needed to hear. My faculty colleague knew I needed to give all my attention to my family and assured me that she would care for our students. A group of colleagues even had a poem in Hawaiian imposed over a photo of my mother and me and framed for my office because they knew I would want to keep an image of her near. They knew how precious my Hawaiian heritage was to me.

These layers of understanding are developed through relationship-building. They come from time spent with one another. They come from learning about and with one another. They also develop as we simply live life and face our trials. While the example of my mother's passing is a somewhat heavy one, it shows how the layers of empathy show up in our lives in meaningful ways every day. Alfred Adler, doctor, psychotherapist, and founder of the school of individual psychology, said, "Empathy is seeing with the eyes of another, listening with the ears of another, and feeling with the heart of another." What are we doing daily to provide these layers and levels of empathy for others? And how much more difficult is it to do so if we passionately disagree with someone? Empathy is not just a matter of listening; it is the very heart of humanity.

Empathy is not just a matter of listening; it is the very heart of humanity.

Remember that Empathy Lens development begins with cultural humility—which takes courage. The development of our Empathy Lens of Humanity starts with a desire to learn from another individual to better understand how they might be experiencing life.

Humanity is grounded in humans understanding other humans and treating them with compassion. It would be disingenuous to claim a desire to live a more humanity-driven life and ignore the work necessary to become more empathetic. The more we try to suspend our deeply held beliefs or notions of the way things are or should be, the more courage it requires of us.

Courageous Empathy

> "It is an act of courageous empathy if you believe you're right but still work to understand the thoughts and feelings of those you disagree with."
>
> —CORY BOOKER, senator

Empathic people are courageous by nature. These individuals are willing to take on the burdens and stresses of others as their own. These are those who understand and feel what others might be feeling. These people set aside time, resources, and energy to learn the challenges someone else might face. Empathy is not a weakness. Rather, it is a courageous act of humanity.

I started this chapter with a few examples of empathy from people close to me or who supported me through a universally painful experience of parental loss. Do I believe it was difficult for them to listen, seek understanding about my feelings, and step in to offer service? I don't think so. Did it still take effort? Yes, but they saw another human suffering and reached out instinctively because of the common understanding of loss. Empathy often requires a bit more effort and courage when it comes to diverse opinions—especially those political in nature. Being empathetic toward someone who shares our experiences, histories, identities, and worldview is easy. We can empathize with individuals who share our ideologies because we think and behave similarly, and our belief systems are aligned. It is much more difficult to have natural empathy for someone we fundamentally disagree with along political and ideological lines. Why is this? Because it is hard to understand why they would believe what they do, and it is even harder to feel how deeply they might feel the impact of certain issues. But learning to do so is worth our effort.

In one of my consultations with a group of community leaders, I was asked to facilitate a conversation between a growing Puerto Rican population and the existing, predominantly White community. At first glance, some might simply call this situation a classic example of culture clash—or the tension that occurs when a minority community from a different culture grows in its size, influence, and voice. However, the more I engaged with the individuals and focus groups, the more I realized that some in the majority lacked the courageous empathy to truly understand the lived experiences and therefore opinions of the growing minority group.

One educational leader, however, demonstrated an increasing aptitude for courageous empathy. At first, he was criticized by a few parents and teachers for not understanding what was needed in terms of translation services, hiring of bilingual staff, transportation support, and after-school programming. I then met and talked with him about putting himself in their situation. What would he do for the success of his children if he felt that the schools weren't helping them succeed? I could see the administrator pause, internalize, and play the scenario in his mind. We talked for a bit more about a prioritized list of actions that could be taken by reallocating existing resources. Then he asked to meet with the same parents and teachers who had been critical of him. We held a follow-up meeting with these parents and teachers and the administrator shared some of his feelings with the group. He initially talked about feeling attacked, believing that the criticisms were born from faulty assumptions about him. He then talked about not fully understanding the depth and breadth of the challenges but that he wanted to understand more. He announced the creation of a new parent–teacher group, with 50 percent representation from the Hispanic (mostly Puerto Rican) community. He talked about hiring some bilingual paraprofessionals to help in the elementary schools. The reaction from the parents and teachers was genuine appreciation. One of the more outspoken teachers even reciprocated by acknowledging that they knew the school was under financial constraints. The responsibility didn't fall solely on the school principal, but the openness to learn and change was most appreciated.

The power of this example is not that the administrator achieved some high level of courageous empathy but rather took a moment to internalize the situation and sought to understand the perspectives of those who disagreed with and criticized him. This example should instill in all of us a sense of optimism, as it signifies that we can strive to enhance our capacity for understanding and empathy.

Being Present to See and Hear

I have facilitated countless dialogues between individuals and groups who seem to talk past one another. We've all experienced this scenario: rather than listening carefully to what is being communicated in words and tone, we are either formulating our thoughts to respond or give advice or simply listening to the words without hearing the message. This happens in just about every relationship at one point or another. We begin to talk *at* one another rather than *with* each other. Being present involves being in the moment with others. It has to do with our ability to not just look at someone and listen to their words but see and hear them.

Much like how experience can shift our lenses or how we view the world, life experiences can shift our ability to hear what someone is sharing. For example, if we have experienced racial discrimination, we might have more empathy when someone tells their own story of racial discrimination. We hear what they say because we process their experience through our memories and feelings of pain. What feelings, histories, and experiences are behind the words being shared? If, through our exposure to such things, we can hear things beyond what is being shared, we have a much deeper ability to be present for someone. Notice the connections with the other lenses of humanity. Before we can ever hope to hear someone properly, we must understand how we might interpret their words through our lenses and the broader context in which such experiences occurred.

There has been significant literature produced on the topic of mindfulness. Such teachings are often rooted in Eastern religious origins of centering oneself and being mindful of thoughts, surroundings, time, and breath. I have found, and research confirms, that people who engage in such practices are slower to anger, more content with their lives and circumstances, and more likely to invest in relationships.

Drawing on such teachings and practice allows each of us to be better prepared to be present for others. In most cases, being present is about asking more questions than giving answers. It means having a genuine curiosity to understand. Questions demonstrate an eagerness to learn, an acknowledgment that the listener wants to truly hear more about the story. It is an admission of a lack of understanding combined with a willingness to learn. The trouble is that far too often, we cannot arrive at such mindful exchanges if we are feeling guilty or defensive.

There is also a big difference between looking at someone and truly seeing them. The phrase "I see you" is often used to signal to someone that the speaker sees much of the context the receiver is navigating. In the university setting, an educator might meet with a student from a first-generation college-bound background, indicating that neither parent nor guardian has completed a bachelor's degree. If the educator indicates that she truly "sees" the first-gen student, she is communicating that she understands the fears, doubts, and questions that the student might have. It signals some level of empathy and will lead the educator to see more deeply into what is needed to help the student succeed. The more exposure we have to diverse identities, experiences, and narratives, the more authentic and prepared we are to truly see people who are different from us. This is not to say that we have become experts on the mindset and experiences of others. Rather, we desire to learn and serve beyond a surface and standard set of practices.

We miss opportunities daily to be present with other people. It is a subtle act that makes a significant difference in the energy between individuals.

We live in an age of *more* and *faster*. We are in constant pursuit of efficiency in life so we can maximize our time. Technology and the convenience culture of consuming goods and experiences have impacted our opportunities to connect meaningfully. Much has been written about the importance of quiet, slowing down, and re-centering ourselves. Think back on the last week. How many meaningful conversations do you think you had? Conversations where both parties were truly listening to one another and engaged with one another? Conversations where you weren't looking at your phone or focused on your next task? Conversations where you walked away appreciating or understanding someone more meaningfully? We miss opportunities daily to be present with other people. It is a subtle act that makes a significant difference in the energy between individuals.

When we want to see and hear one another, we welcome each interpersonal engagement as a learning opportunity, and we begin to understand human communication and interaction as a complex and nuanced experience that requires care and intentionality. Mindfulness invites us to consider how intentional and aware we are of our thoughts, feelings, and experiences. Being present with others invites us to consider how to be intentional and aware of the thoughts, feelings, and experiences of others.

Advocating for Humanity

Every major change I've seen in organizations in my career has been brought about because someone spoke up and someone else listened. Civil rights leader Whitney M. Young Jr. said, "I am not anxious to be the loudest voice or the most popular, but I would like to think that at a crucial moment, I was an effective voice of the voiceless, an effective hope of the hopeless."[1] Humanity-driven lenses are not amoral.

I remember visiting a class to deliver a guest lecture on cultural awareness, understanding, and skills. About thirty minutes into my presentation, a student raised her hand and asked, "So are you saying that we need to try to understand someone who hates us or looks down on us? I don't think I would want to *get to know* Hitler just because I see him as a human. He was an evil person who did evil things. I know not everybody is Hitler, but where is the line between treating people with empathy and recognizing they are not deserving of that empathy?" It was a powerful question, and my answer was quite inadequate. I responded with a flurry of thoughts centered on the fact that we each need to make that judgment for ourselves, and in doing so, we each need to find our moral line.

Since that exchange, I have thought more about that student's question. In many of the world's conflicts, both sides feel justified in their stance, their hatred of the other, and even their need to eliminate the other view. While I am a strong proponent of hearing all sides of issues, this book and the arguments in it reveal my bias that lenses of humanity are rooted not just in the acknowledgment of someone as a human being but in human worth, human dignity, and human respect. I believe we are all inherently born with equal worth as humans, but we are not born into equal circumstances or equal means. The disparity of resources, power, and life opportunities upon birth between individuals has led to an agelong debate about fairness and a balance of the principles of equality vs. equity. We strongly yearn for justice for others and mercy for ourselves. We want fairness through the lenses of our lived experiences and what we perceive to be injustices. We rarely demand fairness when we are in the majority or have an overly disproportionate number of resources.

Humanity requires that we ask ourselves, "To what extent will we use our means and our voices to acknowledge that other humans are deserving of all opportunities life has to offer in its diversity?" If we claim to be humanity-driven, it does not mean we justify why our political party cares more about others. It means our humanity-born empathy requires us to speak up and speak out for all humans to bring their experiences, perspectives, and needs to the table. In other words, humanity-based living and practices focus our energy and efforts on arguments of equity more than focusing simply on equality.

Valuing and *validating* are frequently used interchangeably, but a subtle yet significant distinction exists between them. While expressing that we *value* someone or a group of people, we may acknowledge their worth and appreciate what they offer in a given situation. We may recognize their talents and contributions that benefit our team. However, when we truly value someone, it is crucial to also validate them. *Validation* demonstrates that we believe individuals when they share how they are experiencing the world. Validation goes beyond mere acknowledgment and serves as an affirmation of their perspectives and feelings.

Consider these individuals commonly referred to as embodiments of humanity: Nelson Mandela, Martin Luther King Jr., Mother Teresa. They come to mind not because of their business acumen but because of their unwavering commitment to improving lives and ensuring opportunities for historically marginalized communities. They spent their resources, time, and energy serving and bringing awareness of societal inequities along the lines of race, socioeconomic status, and opportunities for education and overall life dignity. But humanity is not just found in these iconic individuals. It is found any time someone uses their voice to humanize the experiences and perspectives of another and advocates for more humane treatment of other human beings.

CHAPTER SUMMARY

- The heart of humanity is empathy.

- The greater our disposition to see through the eyes of another, the greater our ability to understand their worldview and therefore understand them.

- Courageous empathy is evident when we seek to listen to and understand those we disagree with.

- Being present for others requires intentionality and a desire to learn from them.

- An important component of empathy development and caring connections is our ability to show up for and engage with others. Advocacy for human dignity, human respect, and human rights is a necessary component of a humanity-driven life.

PART 4

The Community Lens

Humanity-driven people connect with and lift groups and communities

Community Lens Snapshot

As humanity-driven people, we recognize and value the importance of communities in our lives. We learn how and why groups of people form and why we feel a part of certain communities and not others. We see communities as sites for connection, bonding, and belonging. We engage in activities that honor our communities—past, present, and future. We become active participants in building communities in more inclusive and welcoming ways. The Community Lens addresses all three areas of human yearning: (1) safety and stability, (2) connection and belonging, and (3) purpose and meaning.

Why a Community Lens?

The heart of human connection is a sense of belonging. We find belonging with individuals (Empathy Lens) and in groups and communities where we are validated (Community Lens). It is difficult to imagine the development and growth of our humanity without a deliberate exploration of how we can impact the greater good. We improve how we show up for our communities as we develop a Community Lens. By utilizing this lens, we will be better prepared and positioned to impact groups of people in more humanity-informed ways. The Community Lens allows us to see people as social and interconnected beings. In our quest to help people find their sense of safety, purpose, and connection, what better way than by lifting groups of people.

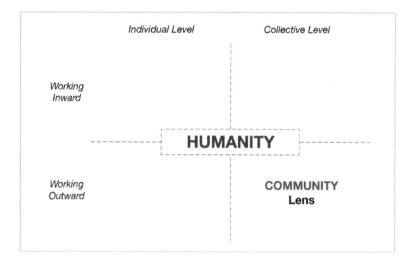

Lenses of Humanity Framework: Community Lens Focus

CHAPTER 10

Canoe One: Honoring the Past: Remember the Communities That Came Before

"It is in the collectivities that we find
reservoirs of hope and optimism."

—ANGELA Y. DAVIS

IN 2017, I WAS ON THE planning committee for the National Association of Multicultural Education conference. Our theme that year focused on the power of our unique identities in education. The committee members asked me to create an art piece that could represent our theme about how our identities impact our notion of community. I was interested in creating a piece that represented how I might help my children think about navigating their futures as mixed-race, mixed-ethnicity individuals.

I started the piece by focusing on a metaphor that could represent the turbulence and messiness of the journey. With my Pacific Islander roots, I found the ocean to be just the right backdrop for a journey through constant turbulence. I knew I wanted to incorporate imagery of the ocean and canoes, as such images resonated with all three of my cultural backgrounds. My Hawaiian, Filipino, and Japanese ancestors were all canoe people. They were the first bridge-builders, as they left their islands to go out, make connections, gather information and resources, and return to their home islands to enrich their communities.

I divided the canvas into two sides, one representing Michele's Navajo heritage and the other representing my Pacific Islander heritage. I used images, patterns, and symbols for both sides that matched our cultural backgrounds. I then placed a canoe in the middle of the piece at an angle with no clear direction of which way it would navigate. As I stared at the whole image, I agonized over what I felt needed to be communicated to my children and the participants of this multicultural education conference. And then it hit me.

Three Canoes: A New Community Framework

I removed the single large canoe and placed three canoes in a row, equally divided between the two cultural sides. I then placed a dot at the center of the middle canoe and spun the canvas. This process created an interesting effect. It didn't matter which canoe (on either side of the middle canoe) was the front or the back. When the piece spun, it showed that no matter what direction you take (or whichever identity you gravitate toward more), you will always have someone or some group that came before you. You will also have someone or some group that will follow you.

I hoped the piece would communicate our responsibility for the past, present, and future regarding the communities we care about and the larger community. As I worked on the image, I thought about my kids, who must each navigate their own journeys of understanding their diverse ancestry. One of the kids might connect more with one of our heritages than the others, and that's OK. In fact, Michele and I have already seen this play out. My primary message to my kids was that they are part of a long line of people within and outside of our family who have influenced how we arrived to where we are today.

I spoke about the art piece at the conference and had quite a few people approach me afterward to tell me how much the metaphor of the three canoes resonated with them and their journeys. There is something powerful about a sense of responsibility to appreciate and serve those you have not met. As we grow in our desire to honor the past, build our present, and prepare for the next generation, we simultaneously grow in our humanity.

Often, we only focus our community efforts on the here and now. We think about what our community needs and how we might become bigger influencers to impact more people. The focus here is to think more holistically. We need to think about community not only in terms of our present groups but also in terms of time and direction. By doing so, we promote the interconnectedness of the human experience from generation to generation and the responsibilities we have in each direction. Each of these three communities (past, present, and future) warrants analysis if we are to take seriously our efforts to develop the Community Lens of Humanity. After all, our yearning for safety, connection, and purpose is often found in communities. The Three Canoes framework invites multigenerational and multidirectional gratitude and community-building.

Canoe One—Those Who Came Before

No one arrived at their current station in life in a vacuum. We should acknowledge that many individuals came before us in our personal, communal, and professional lives to influence how we got to where we are today. Our biggest influencers were often the parents, grandparents, and other guardians who raised us. It was a set of other humans who made decisions that helped create the circumstances of our existence. We honor the humans before us through humanity-based lenses by studying their lives, cultures, languages, and values to inform our own. Not everyone was raised in a loving home environment, and some may not want to remember early family life. Some may have been adopted and not know of specific connections to their birth ancestors. Others have strong connections with their parents and grandparents. The call to honor the past is not only to honor our ancestral lineage. As an educator, I honor the work of those who have removed barriers so that I could enter the profession with more opportunities than they had. I have great respect for those who courageously challenged the status quo so that education would be accessible to all.

We also recognize the interconnectedness and influence of people who have created opportunities in all aspects of our lives. Individuals who helped build the roads we drive on to access resources. People who invented devices to make my life more comfortable or convenient. Ancestors who planted the proverbial trees that have provided me comfort and rest. It is helpful to ask, *What can I do to build a linkage between myself and those who came before me?*

The first canoe invites actions that recognize, connect with, and celebrate the lives of those who came before us and who contributed to improving the human condition. I focus on actions we can take to honor our predecessors so that they might be recognized for their contributions.

Study and Archive

Studying and archiving the lives and contributions of those who came before us connects directly with the Context Lens. The more we learn about the setting and environment of the challenges and struggles, as well as the triumphs and successes, the more we can contextualize and appreciate the work of those who came before.

My maternal grandmother was a prolific journal writer. She wrote in black-and-white Steno notebooks and documented nearly forty years of her life in journal entries. As I read through these journals, I learned more about how my grandmother viewed the world, what was important to her, and the various issues she faced in her day. The grandma I knew growing up was viewed through my lenses as a child, teenager, young adult, and adult. Yes, I saw her in a different light at each of those stages, but to read what she was going through at the same age I am now is a completely different lens shift. She, too, struggled with parenthood, and she, too, had questions about what she was meant to do in this world. My appreciation for her has grown, and although she has passed on and I cannot interview her anymore, I can continue to learn by studying these types of treasured documents.

You may not have ancestors or people in your communities that were as habitual in their journal keeping. However, there may be some records available of family happenings or community notes and events. In my jobs at UVU, I have found records in the form of meeting minutes, archived stories, photos of events, and presidential speeches that have all given me insights into what my professional predecessors faced. Even if the organization you work for is young, you can still study other similar companies or the history of your industry. Doing so will help you better understand how your community or organization arrived at its current state. In national organizations I am a part of, I have studied their origins: Who started it, and why did they feel the need to start such an organization? In both the community I grew up in and the community I currently live in, there are online records of the histories of both. Thankfully, someone has captured some record of the origins of various communities, and we can benefit from them by understanding their growth and evolution. Let us also not forget another connection to our Context Lens: opportunities to read a variety of histories of individuals, organizations, societies, cultures, and communities.

For those without written records or even a written language (some indigenous communities), oral histories must be captured and studied. Interviews with the elders of our communities and those who have retired are treasures that can unlock our deeper understanding of one another. Many indigenous tribes and nations have been losing their native languages due to older generations passing away along with the language, stories, and important cultural knowledge. Part of our collective humanity involves providing resources for various communities to preserve their language. Remember the discussion on the importance of language and naming as they relate to identity. We must support one another in preserving languages that are phasing out, as they are an important connection to the people who came before us.

Some have asked me what they can do if they don't have an exciting history or don't want to study their past, as it is full of trauma and bad memories. I understand the concern and am not advocating that we must study every aspect of our family or community history. But I hope we can find some connection with those who have helped us get to where we are today. It might be a teacher or a coach. It might be a community of musicians or artists. Regardless of the communities that we care about, we can open our hearts to greater humanity by studying their histories, lives, and contributions.

By studying the stories, especially the historically unheard ones, we develop a stronger appreciation for their lived experiences, sacrifices, and impact. Studying historical figures in our families and communities can often present a call to action and motivation for us to continue the work that someone else started. The point is to do something.

By studying the stories, especially the historically unheard ones, we develop a stronger appreciation for their lived experiences, sacrifices, and impact.

Studies on assessment and habit formation have found that whatever you pay attention to improves. If you want to get healthier, we know that paying attention to one's food choices, exercise, rest, and water intake typically lead to healthier outcomes. This is the same for the Context and Community Lenses. As we learn more about contexts, histories, heritage, where we come from, why our grandparents did what they did, or why my predecessor at work did what they did, our understanding, empathy, and relationships improve.

Months after my father passed away, my siblings and I found his videos, photos, and cards he made my mother, and I'm currently working on digitizing them all. Anyone who knows me knows that I take a lot of photos, and I document many things. I do this because I want to feel that sense of connection across generations. When I was the NAME (National Association of Multicultural Education) president for Utah, I knew I was standing on the shoulders of giants (thank you, Charlene Lui and Bette Tate Beaver). I was building off what so many people before me had put together, and my efforts reflected that gratitude. We know that gratitude brings about a great amount of goodwill, good energy, and positivity. My mom was a principal at an alternative/continuation high school in Sun Valley, California. She would talk about her students who returned years after graduation to tell her, "Thank you, Mrs. Reyes. Because of you,

I stayed in school and finished. And when many people had given up on me, you were there." Just learning about this story inspired me to become a champion for my students. Once we have gathered information about people who have impacted our lives and communities, we can find ways to commemorate and celebrate their contributions.

Commemorate and Celebrate

Our responsibility to the communities that have come before also calls us to share their stories. I have seen this done in a variety of ways. Family and life celebrations. Awards and honors named after individuals who helped establish and build the specific community into what it is today. Founders' events acknowledging the impact of visionary leaders. Recognition events bringing people together who have been influenced by a person or organization. No matter the effort, we have elevated humanity and built bridges with the past.

When was the last time you honored the individuals in your family, in your community, or in your organization who contributed to your growth and paved the way for you to stand where you stand? Remember that humanity is helping people feel a sense of connection and purpose. Often, there is a gap in our understanding of how our current work influences future generations. Our efforts to acknowledge that work from the trailblazers in our families, companies, and communities can help bridge this gap and build meaningful connections.

Any time I speak publicly, I first acknowledge my parents. I recognize their stories, their journeys, and their influence on what I hold dear. It is my way of honoring their help in arriving at the very place I am in, with the privilege to speak at that moment. I know that my story is incomplete without understanding their values, cultural backgrounds, and teachings that helped me become who I am. By remembering and celebrating their influences, I have found that my children—even those who hadn't connected deeply with my parents before they passed—can be inspired by their wisdom, life stories, and special characteristics. In Michele's Navajo (Diné) culture, when introducing yourself, you always acknowledge those who came before and declare your family lineage. This is a powerful way to communicate that you are always walking in community with those came before you.

In organizations, the sharing and celebrating of the sacrifices of founders and early leaders can motivate current employees to reconnect with their sense of purpose and be motivated by the courage, hard work, and optimism of people who faced difficulty in creating the company that many now benefit from.

How is your action, activity, event, or service commemorating, celebrating, or validating the community contributions made? How do we honor the humanity of those who have passed the torch to us by ensuring they stay connected and valued?

Imagine how you would feel if someone found a way to celebrate your contributions to your family, your community, or your company. How would you feel if they let you know that your hard work had led to ongoing impact, that people years later were still benefiting from your creativity and your passion? How would it feel for you to be seen for what you have contributed to the world? Now, imagine the gratitude of those who you are celebrating. Each generation assumes that the next generation is a bit more selfish and less appreciative of what it takes to see results. By celebrating and commemorating the contributions of the previous generations, we are honoring their impact on humanity and modeling for others how powerful it can be to lift one another.

Creative Appreciation

One of the great gifts of humanity is gratitude. The more the expression of gratitude is tied to who you are as a person, the more meaningful it becomes. You have unique talents and gifts. With those talents, you have opportunities that are unique to you to express appreciation to the individuals who have impacted you.

As you consider becoming more personal in your efforts toward creative appreciation, don't get overwhelmed—we don't have to honor everybody. Not all people want to honor parents, their bosses, or certain people in their communities. We get to decide which communities and individuals are most meaningful to us. Remember, the purpose is to be authentically appreciative of the contributions of another.

I have decided to connect with people who have helped build the communities I hold dear through shoes. I started designing custom shoes in the summer of 2015 after my mother passed away—first as a healing activity and then as an act of gratitude. I have never sold a pair of my shoes but have been asked multiple times if I can make a special pair for someone to buy. I never got into shoe design to make money and have found that I can't put a price on the shoes, even if I wanted to sell them.

I have decided that designing shoes is a way to honor the influencers in my life that is unique to me, my artistic skills, and my love of shoes. I have designed pairs for my siblings, my wife and kids, former bosses, and people I considered my mentors. My process for making each shoe is very simple: I identify the person I want to make the shoes for and start my research about them. Sometimes I contact someone very close to them or who knows them in a way that I don't so I can glean more insight into their story. I gather information about the person's shoe size, favorite colors, and, most importantly, aspects of their story—cultural elements, language, symbols, interests, words and numbers, and any other information that could inspire a specific design unique to the individual. I then sketch a series of design concepts, testing colors and patterns to communicate a specific story I want to convey. I purchase a pair of shoes that match the person's personality and style, and I work on transferring my design ideas to the shoes. I include some of my cultural patterns in every design to connect us. For me, this whole process can be quite emotional. When I invest this much time into a specific gift for someone, I think about them and their contributions to my life. While each pair of shoes has its own unique story, let me share one example of a pair of shoes that connected me to a mentor who built a community I hold dear.

Pat Hayashi was the first Japanese American to hold a vice-chancellorship in the University of California system. This signals the highest-ranking Asian/Asian American in the history of the famed UC system. Pat was an early leader in forming APAHE—a national organization I belong to that promotes the advancement of Asian Pacific Americans in Higher Education. Pat and I first met when I enrolled in a leadership program in 2014, sponsored by LEAP—a national organization supporting and promoting Leadership Education for Asian Pacifics in all industries. Pat was one of the faculty members and mentors, and immediately upon meeting him, I knew there was much I could learn from him. Over the next few years, we connected often through our mutual love of art, dialogue, and cultural exploration. When I spoke to Pat, I felt I was in the presence of one of my Japanese uncles, who would teach me and share wisdom. During one of our exchanges, I learned that Pat was born in a Japanese internment camp about an hour and twenty minutes from my home in Utah. This greatly impacted me, and when I decided to design a pair of shoes for Pat, I knew the story I wanted to convey. I titled his pair of shoes *Beauty from Pain*. Here is what I said when I presented the pair of shoes to Pat.

The internment of Americans of Japanese ancestry during WWII is one of the worst violations of civil rights against citizens in the history of the United States. The government and the US Army, falsely citing "military necessity," locked up over 110,000 men, women, and children in ten remote camps controlled by the War Relocation Administration and four male-only camps controlled by the Justice Department. These Americans were never convicted or even charged with any crime yet were incarcerated for up to four years in prison camps surrounded by barbed wire and armed guards.

The Topaz Camp was located sixteen miles northwest of Delta in central Utah, on the lip of the Great Basin. Topaz processed 11,212 people through the camp while it was in operation from September 11, 1942, to October 31, 1945. Born in that Topaz camp was Pat Hayashi.

In the three years I have known Pat, I have come to see something that I am sure you all have already seen in your short time with him: he is a gift to those who meet him because he connects with you on your deepest level without you even realizing it. His life, philosophy, and whole being quietly scream, "Beauty from pain." I have felt that Pat's connection with and exploration of his past pain have allowed him to help others work through theirs. I designed a pair of shoes for him to both honor and discover him. I can tell you that I have spent more time, thought, energy, and research on this pair of shoes than any other.

Regarding the design, I start at the back of the shoe. You will notice this seemingly innocuous pattern of repeating vertical and horizontal dashes. These dashes represent the layout of the barracks of the Topaz internment camps and the gate through which Pat entered the world. Around the shoes' "barracks" there is a silver line with small spikes representing the barbed wire that surrounded the barracks. If you look closely, there is a number on the back of each shoe. The numbers 32 and 25 represent the ages of Pat's father, Henry, and his mother, Aiko, when their family was forcibly relocated. I start from the back of the shoe because it represents Pat's painful entrance into this world—his past, not his future. As Pat steps forward, this image will never leave him, but it doesn't have to be his focus moving forward.

Moving on to the sides of the shoes, we have the rising sun. These two suns represent Pat's choices throughout his life, to either allow the sun to set on his opportunities or to view the sun and his future rising. In other words, these sister images are reminders that there will be dark days and bright days in our lives, but we ultimately have the choice to take advantage of opportunities placed before us and to look at the horizon with hope.

You will also notice that the sunrays carry over to the other side of the shoe. But these sunrays, when looked at independently, have the look of prison uniform stripes. At the bottom of one of the stripes, you will notice Pat's parents' actual internment record number. The number reads 20284. Pat's father, Henry, had 20284-A, and Pat's mother, Aiko, had 20284-B. This symbol is a reminder that even though Pat's family eventually left Topaz, the prison experience was a memory that stayed with them. This image, tied to the rising and setting suns, invites us to think about how we might turn painful memories into something hopeful.

On the front of the shoe is an image of a cherry blossom tree. The cherry blossom, or *sakura*, is the national flower of Japan and carries several symbolic interpretations, including a graceful acceptance of destiny and karma, Japanese pride, and volatile clouds that rest in the heavens.

This image represents many things I love about Pat. It represents his Japanese heritage as well as a symbol of serenity and peace. It represents a place where young Japanese children can learn at the feet of their wise parents, grandparents, ancestors, and elders. This is what Pat makes people feel, despite whatever turbulence may be going on in our hearts and minds. When you are with Pat, you are with wisdom, peace, and hope. It represents the artistic voice he found later in life and the colorful and rich vibrancy that he adds to his relationships. The ways he challenges each of us to look at the world around us with new lenses and new perspectives. It represents growth. It symbolizes that hope and beauty can grow from painful pasts and experiences.

Finally, on the side of the right shoe, you will see identical designs that look like a lowercase *t* and an upside-down *v*. Each one of these figures is the Japanese kanji for *wood* or *tree*. When the two symbols are together, they represent *woods* or *forest*. This is the meaning of *Hayashi*. Next to these symbols are written the names Aiko and Henry. You will notice that Pat's parents are with him in every phase of his life journey. They are no longer the focal point of his life, but they create a full circle of connection with his ancestors. I put their names next to the Hayashi kanji to represent that his parents were the two strong trees of his life.

Pat, thank you for being so generous with all of us. You are a gift to this world, and we are blossoming because of your influence. We love you and honor you. Mahalo.

This was how I wanted to show creative appreciation for someone who has opened doors for me. In what ways can you show creative appreciation that is unique, authentic, and meaningful to you? Creativity is not just artistic. Creativity is about bringing something into existence—an idea, a solution, a product, a story. Creative appreciation involves using your unique talents or gifts to help someone know how grateful you are for them. How do we express our gratitude to those who have built our communities? We get to know them and try to express our gratitude in a way that can show them that we have put thought and care into our appreciation.

As we study and archive, celebrate and commemorate, and creatively show appreciation to past generations, we are building community. We are helping individuals feel connected and valued. We are elevating humanity for many who thought they and their contributions were forgotten.

Creative appreciation involves using your unique talents or gifts to help someone know how grateful you are for them.

Take Action: Creative Appreciation

1. Make a list of people who have helped you get to where you are today or who have helped build the programs or organizations you value or had an impact on your life. These names can be in different categories:

    a. Family: parents, guardians, grandparents, other ancestors who have influenced who you are today

    b. Friends/Community: individuals who have mentored you or lifted the communities you hold dear

    c. Professional: those who have provided professional support, leadership, and mentoring to help you get to where you are professionally

    d. Religious/Spiritual/Ideological: people who have been spiritual guides or those who have influenced your values and connections to a higher purpose or power

2. Select one individual and choose an expression of creative appreciation that is personal to you. Find a way to deliver such gratitude to the individual in a way that allows for

meaningful exchange. Help them see the influence they have had on you and how you are building on or expanding their work or impact.

CHAPTER SUMMARY

- The concept of three canoes—situating ourselves always in the middle canoe—invites a recognition of our communities past, present, and future. The Three Canoes framework allows us to be deliberate in building community in multiple directions.

- There are a variety of ways we can build community with those who have come before.

- Study and archive: our efforts to learn about and document the contributions of our predecessors provides greater context of appreciation and signals to them how much we care about their impact and legacy.

- Commemorate and celebrate: after we've learned about the contributions of those who came before, we should find ways to publicly acknowledge them not only for their benefit, but to signal that you will always appreciate the contributions of previous generations.

- Creative appreciation: utilize your unique skills, talents, and creativity to demonstrate appreciation for someone who helped you get to where you are today. The fact that it will be an expression unique to you will make it more meaningful.

CHAPTER 11

Canoe Two: Engaging the Present: Impact Your Current Communities

"If you want to go quickly, go alone.
If you want to go far, go together."

—AFRICAN PROVERB

ON MARCH 11, 2020, I SAT in the Orleans Arena in Las Vegas, awaiting the women's basketball game to start our university run in the Western Athletic Conference (WAC) tournament, but the tension in the air was not from the anticipated matchup. COVID-19 had been spreading in pockets around the world, and just one month earlier, the World Health Organization (WHO) declared a global health emergency due to nearly ten thousand cases and two hundred deaths. One week before the WAC tournament, twenty-one people on a cruise ship off the California coast tested positive for COVID. Some athletic conferences had already canceled their tournaments earlier that week, and there were questions about what the WAC would do. While waiting for our game to start, I received an ESPN alert on my phone indicating that Rudy Gobert had just tested positive for COVID-19, and the Utah Jazz were suspending their game. Ten minutes later, another alert indicated that the NBA had suspended their season indefinitely. Twenty minutes later, the NHL announced the suspension of their season. Our game was then canceled, and by 10 p.m., WAC officials announced that the rest of the tournament was canceled. Two days later, on March 13, 2020, President Trump declared the novel coronavirus a national emergency.

In the days that followed, nearly every sector of our lives was shut down in an unprecedented way. Schools, churches, businesses, and other services paused to assess and then tried to move virtually, wherever possible. Almost overnight, platforms like Zoom, Skype, Microsoft Teams, Cisco Webex, and Google Meet were overwhelmed with demands on bandwidth, usability, and expansion of services. Challenges began to compound as parents became teachers, childcare facilities shut down, revenue halted, and hospitals started filling. Jobs were lost as businesses and organizations closed shop. Masks became our standard accessory. And you remember the long lines hoping for lottery-style luck to see if toilet paper, hand sanitizer, and sanitizing wipes were still available. While there is much to unpack about various lessons learned from the COVID-19 pandemic, my focus is on its effect on community.

Our Need for In-Person Connection

Our sense of community was disrupted dramatically, and for the first six months, much of the world was in triage mode. There was no time for long-term strategic planning or even short-term planning; we were collectively reacting to every new challenge and twist brought on by the pandemic.

When we struggle with something in our lives, we hope to have people to turn to who are on more solid ground. When we're down, they might be up and can lift us in our time of need as we reciprocate in their time of need. COVID took away networks of comfort and support, as everyone needed to take care of themselves in dealing with uncertainty.

The shutdowns resulted in physical isolation and a mindset of taking care of our own as we navigated the ambiguity and unexpected obstacles that came our way. I didn't want to bother my neighbor or friend because they, too, were dealing with their share of stress. I didn't want to contribute further to their burdens during this trying time.

When we tried to replicate our existing connections online, it was difficult, and the feeling wasn't the same. I was part of a planning committee to prepare for a conference in Long Beach in November 2020. When COVID first hit the US, we thought it would pass, and for the first couple of months, we stayed the course with our in-person conference plans. As the months dragged on, it became very clear that the world would not open back up, and budgets were being cut because of lost revenue from offices shutting down.

I remember a very specific conversation we had as a planning committee. About twenty-five of us were on a virtual call, and everyone shared what they thought we should do. After a few general comments, someone said, "Look, it kills me to recommend this, but I think we need to pivot to a virtual platform now and plan for the best virtual conference we can. Even if we were to have it in person, people wouldn't have the budget, nor would their institutions allow them to travel." After that comment, you could see the dampening effect it had. Most everyone agreed that moving to a virtual platform was the right decision. Still, you could tell it was sinking in that we wouldn't gather together. A few got emotional and said, "I joined this organization because it felt like a family, and we had these connections." You could tell that people were exhausted from dealing with stuff in their state, and it was difficult to come out of that.

How did COVID-19 affect your sense of community, and what did you learn about yourself and your community's needs? Through focus groups and conversations with how others have experienced this pandemic, here are some lessons I learned about our sense of community:

- We didn't realize how much we valued in-person connection until we were mandated not to have it.

- There is something powerful about physical contact that we take for granted, including handshakes, hugs, and simply sharing physical space.

- Virtual meeting fatigue is real! While convenient and efficient, there is something limiting about our ability to fully feel a sense of community and togetherness.

- Many have reassessed their level of happiness in their current jobs or have been forced to look for new career and learning opportunities, thus introducing new communities and self-analyses of what we want out of our work life. For the good of mental health, we need to find a strong combination of in-person and virtual connections.

While we have seen improvements in our new normal of a hybridized life, it is clear that we are missing something if we do not get together. At the university, there is a big difference between online and in-person classroom experiences when it comes to building a sense of community.

I don't argue that virtual platforms cannot offer points of meaningful connection. In fact, video conferencing platforms can lend themselves to some level of human connection that would not happen otherwise, due to distance and time. That said, regarding our efforts to build a sense of community, we need to be intentional about creating in-person moments for engagement. Organizations with a strong culture facilitate in-person, face-to-face interactions that can create more engagement and build greater trust. In-person interactions provide "watercooler" moments of informal connection that develop trust without feeling forced. In virtual communications and gatherings, participants become distracted, feel less responsibility to be present, and may have difficulty reading the room or picking up on nonverbal cues.

To be clear, hybridization (virtual and in-person engagement) in community-building is the new norm. Every day, we create and adopt new technologies that improve efficiency, productivity, and, yes, even connection. But let us also be just as creative in finding ways to gather for moments of deeper, in-person connection.

Mine, Yours, and Ours

I have been and still am a part of many communities. I feel connected to the geographical communities of the San Fernando Valley in Southern California (where I grew up) and Utah County in the heart of the Beehive State (where I live now). I am rooted in cultural communities of my native Hawaiian, Filipino, and Japanese ancestors and family members, as well as the Native American (Navajo/Diné) cultural community of my wife. I have always resonated with various art communities with a special connection to urban arts of graffiti, hip-hop, street dance, and spoken word. I have loved my professional community of educators at K–12 and college/university levels. I have grown up feeling a strong sense of responsibility to and engagement with diverse religious communities. And yes, I have my "nerd" communities of LA sports fandom, comic books, vintage toys, and cinema collectibles. We are all part of a variety of communities. Why? Because we yearn for a sense of connection and belonging.

So what is our charge? We need to understand, lift, and serve our communities and the broader human community—including some we may not have strong connections with. Robert Putnam, in his book titled *Our Kids: The American Dream in Crisis*, recommends a reimagining of the conversation around the students we care about. He argues that we shouldn't divide students between "my kids" and "their kids" but that we should see all students as "our kids." He continues by inviting us all to stop the American political division of red vs. blue and to consider the crumbling of the American Dream as a purple problem.[1] Humanity doesn't demand that we only treat those in our communities with respect. Putnam's challenge should be a part of our daily reflection. It beckons us to treat all humans with respect, dignity, and compassion.

As the fourth lens of humanity, the Community Lens is driven by a sense of responsibility to the collective. Our humanity is not meant solely for our individual growth or the growth of only two people. It is meant to build and lift communities of humans and to improve the sense of safety, purpose, and belonging for more individuals.

I am fascinated by how quickly our collective humanity can show up in the face of a major natural disaster or in a heinous act that is universally despised. Why is it that we can set aside differences and allegiances to specific communities for a brief moment to come together and mourn as one human community? During natural disasters worldwide (think Haiti, Myanmar, Philippines, and Indonesia), the global community came together to support the affected people with physical and financial resources, prayers, and verbal empathy. Immediately following September 11, 2001, the United States (and global empathizers) put everything on hold. For a few months, there seemed to be a stall in divisiveness, pettiness, and rancor. Temporarily, our humanity showed through when we reached out to individuals we didn't even know to comfort and console them. Sadly, such humanity quickly dissipates with the layers of politics, social media, religious turmoil, and fear resuming their hold on society. It's as if our comfort from collectively seeing one another as humans is limited to moments of human suffering. I believe this happens because, for all our differences of opinion, we are generally empathetic creatures who don't want to see people suffer.

Rather than wait for such tragedies to occur, how can we see one another through eyes of compassion, empathy, and consideration, even in the face of disagreement? Think about a moment when you made a negative judgment about a person, learned new information about their life situation, immediately felt empathy for them, and changed your position. This has happened to me many times. I might be frustrated with someone and then hear some of their struggles and that their lack of attention to my issue is due to good reason. My lenses shift, and my judgment subsides. We need more interactions to give people the benefit of the doubt. Isn't that what we wish people would give to us?

If we are to truly move away from "mine vs. yours" to a focus on "ours," we need to shift from the focus on the individual to thinking of the collective.

From Leadership to Communityship

In his *Harvard Business Review* article titled "Rebuilding Companies as Communities," Henry Mintzberg outlines why organizations must revisit their intentionality to build community. The article, published in 2009 during the Great Recession, states that "beneath the current economic crisis lies another crisis of far greater proportions: the depreciation in companies of community—people's sense of belonging to and caring for something larger than themselves."[2] Mintzberg proposed the adoption of the word *communityship* as a necessary companion in any conversation about leadership. Leadership, while still important, focuses on the impact of individual leaders. Communityship recognizes collective skills, knowledge, talents, and perspectives and promotes a much more distributed model of influence that engages the whole ecosystem of the organization.

But let's be careful before we label an organization as humanity-driven if its own culture does not value the contributions, innovations, and voices of the very humans working there.

Before an organization can become humanity-driven, its leaders need to value the concept of communityship as an essential component. An organization might tout their humanitarian efforts, but let's be careful before we label an organization as *humanity-driven* if its own culture does not value the contributions, innovations, and voices of the very humans working there.

Another of Robert Putnam's famous texts, *Bowling Alone*, chronicles the erosion of community gatherings and connections. He argues that bowling league participation is emblematic of the erosion of social gatherings, as fewer and fewer people bowl in leagues and teams each year. He offers a call of caution for all who feel more connected (perhaps through technology) but are less involved in actual sociality through communities.[3] We develop a false sense of connection with the volume of likes, loves, and emojis but still feel more and more isolated due to a lack of deeper, more meaningful engagements with one another.

An appropriate metaphor is the American corporate boardroom with a long skinny table with the CEO at the head of it. When I was introduced to tribal leadership in the Navajo Nation, I visited their chapter houses and was struck by their council chambers and the shape of their circular conference table. While certain people are designated to be leaders, there is something visually symbolic about not having anybody at the head of the table. Many organizations I have worked with, where women are the leaders, have redesigned their spaces to be more holistic and less like a traditional executive space. It's an important discussion, one that is rooted in the collective rather than the individual.

The study of community and communities needs to be elevated in our organizations and given at least as much attention as the focus on leadership development. In a time when the problems that face individuals, organizations, and societies are more complex than ever, it will take an engaged and diverse community to generate the type of solutions that are needed. Onboarding new employees or participants into our organizations is an important opportunity to establish a culture of communityship, where all feel like they are adding value and contributing.

Personal Passion Partnerships

We reside in layers of communities and interconnectedness. There are ways we benefit from the existence of communities without even recognizing it. Someone might benefit from a paved road even though they are unsure who paved it or how it was paid for. That same person pays local taxes and counts on others in the neighborhood to do the same so that all might benefit from sanitation services, schools, parks, and overall safety and support. The unseen reciprocity is a powerful part of our responsibility to our communities. As part of our unwritten social agreements with one another, we make sacrifices and receive benefits. I can influence this ecosystem that we call our community and benefit from one influenced by my neighbor. Once again, the mutually beneficial partnership is evident.

Each of us has things that we are passionate about. I don't mean that everyone demonstrates their passion in the same way, but we all have things that we care about. One of my favorite activities is sitting with a young adult who expresses a lack of direction in their life. As a former college and career adviser, I felt like my responsibility was to help each student unpack and analyze their innate talents and interests and guide them to consider a menu of opportunities. When asked about their college major or a career of interest, many young people say, "I don't know." Perhaps you have said the same thing at some point in your life. My invitation is to simply have a conversation with someone about things that are important to you. Don't focus on college or career. Focus on the impact you want to have on your community.

There are a number of ways to do this. Here is a list of brainstorming questions and prompts to consider as you reflect on the impact you want to have on the world around you.

- Who are individuals you care about and why? What impact do you want to have on them?

- What are communities or groups you care about and why? What impact do you want to have on them?

- What have people told you are your talents, skills, and abilities?

- In what ways could these talents, skills, and abilities help individuals or communities?

- Who are people you admire who are making an impact on the communities or causes you care about?

- What do they do to make an impact?

- How might you partner with them to make an impact on the communities and causes you care about?

- What would you need to be successful in making an impact?

- How much time could you dedicate to contributing to your personal passion project?

By personally writing answers to these questions or dialoguing with someone about them, we unlock possibilities for personal passion partnerships that we can engage in to build community. We can get involved with our local community. We can take on a leadership role in some organization we care about. Communities are built by individuals working together for a common purpose. And remember, we may not even realize that our passions can make a difference.

Something I used to avoid but have now embraced is the need to fundraise for the things I'm passionate about. About eight years ago, I sat with our vice president of advancement at the university (senior administrator for fundraising), and I told him of my hesitancy to fundraise. He asked me what I was passionate about at UVU. I told him I was passionate about equitable educational opportunities for all students—especially those who have historically had limited access to higher education. He then asked me to talk more about the specifics. He urged me to talk about the needs and what solutions I would bring if I had the resources to do so. I talked with him about scholarships, programming services, engaged learning activities and opportunities, centers and physical space needs, and the transformational power of education. When I was done talking, he said, "Well, you sold me. You just fundraised." I laughed and told him, "I don't think so. I was just telling you about my passions and the needs we have." He then said, "What do you think fundraising is? It's about storytelling and matching a need with someone who has the desire and means to help with that need." I was stunned and never looked at fundraising the same again. I am not proposing that you become a fundraiser; I simply invite you to consider what it means to proactively ask people to engage with and support things you are passionate about.

We develop a healthy attitude of engagement when we want something improved. For about four years, I participated in a statewide multicultural task force. During one of my first meetings, a committee member offered some harsh critique of the state government and whether it was committed to true inclusion and equity. As a new committee member, I didn't mind the critique. In fact, I welcomed that sort of candor in our meetings and was excited to share my voice similarly, if warranted. But then something happened. The chair turned to this committee member and said, "Thank you for raising that. What ideas or recommendations do you have to address this issue?" The person hesitated and responded, "Well, I'm not the expert here." I was a bit stunned. I didn't expect the committee member to have a fully formed proposal, but I also didn't expect them to deflect any responsibility to be a part of the solution.

It can be very easy in politics and organizations to critique what we feel is not being done. I know because I've done it. I find things all the time that I'd like to change. But I have learned that complaining without plans, ideas, or energy to address the situation has not yielded meaningful results. I have found that those who show up with some solutions and recommendations can make the change happen more quickly. This happens for a few reasons.

But I have learned that complaining without plans, ideas, or energy to address the situation has not yielded meaningful results.

First, an obvious connection exists between an actual idea or proposal and the fact that people (leaders, committee members, public) can respond to that proposal. If more people like it, it tends to go through more quickly. If people don't like it, it probably needs refinement or additional advocates. Either way, by bringing a solution to address the problem, there is a higher likelihood that something will be done.

Second, it reveals right away to the proposer what the obstacles are. I have witnessed great proposals blocked because of new information about limited resources, time frames, or political dynamics. Over my twenty-plus years in higher education, I have brought dozens of solutions to thorny problems. Not all of them followed my proposed solutions, but nearly all of them caused some form of change. Sometimes, if the solution is not supported, the process reveals how I might approach things differently.

Third, there is a general assumption that the person bringing the solution forward is trying to improve the experiences of individuals within the organization or community. Critique without ideas to address the issues comes across as immature complaining, and organizations and communities don't want to be surrounded by people who only complain about their communities without trying to improve them.

There are countless ways we can each become involved in the communities we care about. Humanity-driven people engage with and lift communities. The key is setting aside time and being intentional about the impact we want to have.

Take Action: Community Impact Vision Boarding

I have long been a fan of the power of vision boards and the effect they can have on my motivation, drive, and behavior. Let me return to the power of information received visually by our brains. Vision boards (in all their variations) create a visual imprint on the mind and are coded in our brains. The more such images are imprinted on our minds, the more our brains believe that achieving such a vision is possible. Remember, in advertising and political campaigning, images can create emotions, which vary along the spectrum between attraction (that looks appetizing) and repulsion (that candidate looks shady). These images get filed away in our mental boxes with some element of a positive or negative emotion. The stronger the emotions tied to a particular experience or image and the frequency of seeing it, the more significant the impact on shaping our future behavior.

Vision boards are predicated upon one's desire to bring good things into their life by increasing the frequency of encounters with visual imprints. With all of life's distractions, the vision board helps keep certain priorities at the forefront of our minds. Therefore, hopefully, it affects how we live in some self-fulfilling prophecy. Deliberate exposure to new visual elements can have an impact on the way we normalize difference and diversity. Visual encounters can also lead to more meaningful engagement opportunities for learning.

We already use visual cues in our everyday lives. We decorate our homes and our workspaces with visual reminders of various things, including our values, memories, family, interests, cultural heritage, mentors, meaningful quotes, hobbies, and more. All of these serve to provide us a sense of comfort, familiarity, and connection. They also serve to remind us of our accomplishments (diplomas), support network (photos), lifestyle (plants), and journey (childhood artifacts). But how often do we also surround ourselves with visual cues about our goals, our aspirations, and the impact we want to have on the world around us?

There are some things to consider as you develop your community impact vision board:

- Vision boards usually consist of images and words that you connect with

- Transfer your community impact goals to your device(s)

- Create short-term community impact goals that lead to big goals

- Schedule time in your calendar to work on your community impact goals

- Give yourself an incentive/treat when you make progress on your community impact goals

- Combine goals (time with kids + service in the community = serving in the community with kids)

- Determine what you want the images and words to motivate you to do

- Change your habits and systems to force progress toward your community impact goals

- Engage in a community of people with similar goals

- Don't feel like you need to put everything on your vision board

Your community impact vision board can be done digitally, or you can make one physically. The point is to have it in a place where you know you will see it often. I believe that as you develop your community impact vision board, it will serve as a constant reminder of the type of difference you can make in your communities.

CHAPTER SUMMARY

- COVID-19 impacted every aspect of our lives, including the connections with our communities. We learned of the importance of in-person connection experiences as vital for community-building. We bond more meaningfully as we experience things together.

- As we think about our responsibility to build community, let's not only focus on our clique areas or comfort communities. We should both build our current communities and find ways to build broader communities that require us to stretch a bit to learn.

- Our organizations need to shift the focus from leadership development to community development or from leadership to communityship. This approach centers the collection of individuals as the focus of engagement rather than one or a few leaders.

- We can find meaningful ways to build our current communities by identifying personal passion projects and inviting people to get involved.

- A community impact vision board can be a helpful and regular reminder of the impact you want to have in your communities.

CHAPTER 12

Canoe Three: Building the Future: Strengthen Communities with and for the Next Generation

"The greatness of a community is most accurately measured by the compassionate actions of its members."

—CORETTA SCOTT KING

AT THE END OF EACH SEMESTER, I typically conduct an activity called the Life Book exercise. I hand out Steno notebooks to the students and invite them to visualize how the book might contain their life story. Each page represents a year of their lives, and I ask them to count out the pages or years that they have lived. With the diverse age range in my classes, they typically count out between nineteen and fifty pages. I then invite the class to imagine all of the experiences and names that are captured in their life books. I invite them to consider the names that impacted their lives, positively or negatively. Each person then shares with a neighbor the name of a person who has helped them get to where they are. Someone who has encouraged them and supported them along their journey. They each share for a few minutes the impact of their chosen person and then we bring the group together for broader sharing. Inevitably, as stories are told, smiles emerge, some tears are shed, and vulnerability is present. The feelings of connection and gratitude are deep and powerful.

We then switch up the exercise. I invite them to consider the life books of their students. I ask them to choose a student (K–12) in their mind and count out the pages of their age. We then focus on the pages that have yet to be filled in and the stories that have yet to be written. Let me shift to speak to you now as if you were one of my students.

> Consider for a moment the impact you will have on the lives of these young people. As one of their teachers, whether you like it or not, your name will show up in their life books. Will your name be associated with positive entries or negative ones? How often will your name show up? When people look back on their lives and are asked to identify a mentor, supporter, or someone who encouraged them to get where they are, will your name come to mind?
>
> In order for your name to be a positive entry in the life books of others, you have to be intentional about it. And please recognize the power you have as an educator to validate and value each student in their uniqueness. You did not sign up to merely teach material. You opted in to a profession that empowers other humans to find their voices, develop their talents, tell their stories, and connect with the unique contributions they

can make on society. You make dreams happen—or, at least, you have the opportunity to do so. And unfortunately, not all teachers share this vision. They lose sight of what is at the core of the role of a teacher—to teach in a way that helps others to love learning. To care for young people and encourage them to reach their potential. To believe in them even if they don't believe in themselves or lack a strong support network. Teachers make every other career possible, and your influence not only can leave a positive entry in their life books but can also become an entire chapter that they return to for strength.

In order for your name to be a positive entry in the life books of others, you have to be intentional about it.

After some variation of this speech, we discuss ways they can be intentional about becoming a positive influence on the next generation. Our community extends far beyond the here and now. A vital part of any community is the next generation who will inherit it. Our decisions now should be selflessly tied to the futures they will have. The final canoe in multidirectional community-building is a call to lift those who will follow us.

Communities are essential structures of human life and human connection. They provide a place for belonging, common interests, and relationships. They help formulate a sense of identity and place, including geographical ties. Communities are where feelings of trust and understanding can be developed. Conversely, a lack of community is where we can feel isolation, loneliness, and despair. If we are not intentional about helping the next generation develop a sense of community and become a contributing part of their communities, we miss an opportunity to help them develop their own lenses of humanity.

The Growth of Loneliness with Each Generation

According to a 2020 Cigna survey, younger generations report feeling more loneliness than older generations.[1] Seventy-nine percent of Gen Zers, 71 percent of Millennials, and 50 percent of Boomers reported loneliness. Loneliness in Americans is up 7 percent, from 54 percent in 2018 to 61 percent in 2020. Additional data from that report indicate the following:

- Americans reporting good mental health is down five percentage points, from 81 percent in 2018 to 76 percent in 2020.

- Key determinants of loneliness in America:
  ◦ Lack of social support and infrequent meaningful social interactions
  ◦ Negative feelings about one's relationships
  ◦ Poor physical and mental health
  ◦ A lack of "balance" in one's daily activities—doing too much or too little of anything

According to American Psychological Association writer Amy Novotney, there is a distinction between loneliness and social isolation. "Loneliness is not synonymous with chosen isolation or solitude. Rather, loneliness is defined by people's levels of satisfaction with their connectedness, or their perceived social isolation."[2]

The same Cigna report highlights the following alarming data regarding loneliness in the workplace:

- People who report that they don't have good relationships with coworkers (53.7 percent) are ten points lonelier than those who do (43.7 percent).

- Lonely workers report being twice as likely to miss a day of work due to illness and five times as likely to miss a day of work due to stress.

- In an average month, lonely workers report that they think about quitting their job more than twice as often as non-lonely workers.

In addition to these data, loneliness and social isolation affect our lives in profound ways, including heightened health risks, with increases in smoking and alcohol-use disorders, depression, poor sleep quality, impaired executive function, accelerated cognitive decline, dementia, poor cardiovascular function, and impaired immunity at every stage of life. Social isolation also increases the risk of premature death for every cause and race. Social connection is vital to prevent cognitive and emotional decline as people age.

These findings are troubling, and the trend is not going in the right direction. How did we get here? What has led to and continues to influence the increase in loneliness and feelings of social isolation? There are a variety of factors, including some demographic shifts. More than a quarter of the US population lives alone—the highest rate ever recorded. The number of people marrying and having children steadily declines each year. Technology has created efficiencies that have led to fewer human engagements (just think of your shopping experience today compared to twenty or even ten years ago). A more complex and mixed society regarding race, ethnicity, gender identity, language, sexual orientation, and varying other identities, while rich with learning opportunities, has led to more complex social navigation.

As we consider developing a stronger Community Lens of Humanity, let us remember our goal. Our humanity is found in helping others find a sense of safety, purpose, and connection. Psychiatric mental health nurse practitioner Jody Schoenecker said, "Being connected to others socially is widely considered a fundamental human need—crucial to well-being and survival."[3]

We may not always be able to articulate it to one another, but we crave connection, relationships, intimacy, dialogue, validation, and being a part of something bigger than ourselves. If we are to reverse the trends of increased loneliness with each generation, we must engage them, listen to them, and create ways for them to contribute to community-building.

Social Media: Building Community or Exacerbating the Problem

We cannot have a conversation about community-building with the next generation without discussing the impacts of social media on human connection, communication, and relationships. While most studies that sought to assess social media's effects on depression, loneliness, and anxiety have been correlational in their conclusions, recent studies have found more causality.[4]

There are various ways social media creates more tension than opportunities for understanding.

- **More access to comparison culture**—Children at a younger and younger age who engage in social media see what they do and do not have. The FOMO (fear of missing out) culture on social media is real. It is difficult to place a value on something in a vacuum. In other words, so much of how we place value on things depends on how rare it is, how unique it is, and who has access to it. We've seen this phenomenon play out hundreds of times. Social media and the engagement of followers and likes have had such an impact on the mental health of youth that entire countries are now blocking the "like" feature to lessen the popularity focus and allow participants to zero in on more meaningful engagement through comments.

- **Increased shallow connection but not a tight sense of community**—Facebook, Instagram, Twitter, and other platforms have undoubtedly increased a sense of digital connection in a way that physical letters could not achieve. The accessibility of real-time updates, photos, and interactions has undeniably facilitated connections between individuals in ways that were once considered unimaginable. However, it is important to acknowledge that these digital connections often span many individuals but tend to lack depth or intimacy.

- **Reinforced echo chambers and tribalism**—The final false promise of social media is the feeling that we have more exposure to diversity of thought than we do. Yes, it is true that, through certain platforms, we have exposure to how someone with different ideologies might feel about a certain issue. Still, our engagement (or lack thereof) with that person makes a difference in our understanding of diverse thoughts. Social media platforms are not set up for meaningful dialogue and engagement—especially across differences.

We need to be intentional about finding the benefits of both the virtual and in-person formats to engage community. As we work with those of the next generation, we need to also create opportunities for them to practice meaningful dialogue, engagement, and critical inquiry. We also need to model what it means to create or build community as we grow in our careers and lives.

Our Names in the Life Books of Others

Remember my invitation to my students during the Life Book exercise? I invited them to consider how they might be intentional in showing up as a positive entry in the life books of their students. Over the years, I have heard a variety of wonderful ideas from my students about how they might build community with and for the next generation. The "next generation" does not necessarily mean people who are younger than us. It may be people who are new to the field or the organization or simply who join our teams. The ideas below are not simply for K–12 educators or for senior leadership. These are more general recommendations we can consider in an effort to pay it forward.

1. **Mentoring, coaching, and sponsoring**—One of the key ways we can act upon our responsibility to the next generation is to be deliberate about carving out time for mentoring, coaching, guiding, and sponsoring. We all can mentor and be mentored. For the past twelve years, I have participated as a faculty member in a series of leadership development programs at the institutional and national levels. It was not too long ago that I was the one attending many of these leadership development programs and seeking mentors. Our programmatic discussions have identified mentors from all backgrounds, ages, relationships, identities, and professions. Some were more traditional mentors (parents or supervisors), while others were informal and unexpected (coworkers,

friends, children, etc.). Every time we discuss the mentors in our lives, I am struck by how much participants gain from even the most minor of mentoring moments. It reminds me each time that if we can be a bit more deliberate in looking up from our lives and reaching out to someone to see where they are headed, we can profoundly impact dozens of lives.

2. **Connect them to your networks**—Every time we make ourselves available to provide a listening ear, advice, or advocacy, we are validating the next generation to feel and be a part of something. When we open our networks to others, we generate a greater sense of commitment to the collective. We also forget that our networks, which seem so normal now, have been earned over time and have often not been accessible to everyone. As a young professional, how meaningful is it for you to be introduced to people more seasoned and experienced than you—especially if they take an interest in helping you grow? By connecting the next generation to your networks, you are empowering them with opportunities for exposure, engagement, and growth. Conversely, and in the spirit of reciprocity, they also learn to connect you with their networks so that you have a better sense of how the next generation thinks and what is important to them.

3. **Engage them in community causes and capacity-building**—Each new generation seems more cause-driven. Surveys of Millennials and Gen Zers find that they are very purpose-driven. They want to make a difference in the world but do not have the patience to work in systems that don't allow them to make that difference quickly. So, find creative ways to get young people involved in and engaged with the

improvement of communities they care about. This assumes that you are aware of and engaged with community causes yourself. Exposure to opportunities to lift our communities can create a habit of community-building for all involved. The more people can get involved, take on responsibilities, and see results, the greater their confidence and willingness to continue staying involved.

There are many more ways to build community with the next generation. The point is to be deliberate about it. This type of community-building does not come naturally to most. It requires some additional effort. But as we build time for these, and other activities, we develop humanity-driven habits that will have a lasting effect on our communities for generations to come. Building community forward means that we ask ourselves, *What am I doing for the next generation?* My utmost aim is to help individuals who perceive a lack of opportunities in their lives become aware that I am fully dedicated to advocating for them. We have discussed the importance of showing up in people's life books, and on a personal level, I strive for each entry I make in someone's life book to be filled with positive experiences. I want to be a source of support, offering encouragement, positivity, understanding, and an unwavering commitment to their humanity, dignity, and overall well-being.

CHAPTER SUMMARY

- Each new generation reports higher levels of loneliness than previous generations. This is influenced by technology and the increase of social engagements virtually rather than in person.

- Social media has the opportunity to both build community and exacerbate isolation and loneliness. We need to recognize that the next generations need to be taught how to engage in more direct, personal, and meaningful ways.

- We need to be intentional about how we help build community with the next generations. We will show up in their life books, for good or for bad. It takes deliberate effort to mentor the next generation, connect them to your networks, and engage them in community causes.

Conclusion

CHAPTER 13

Living the Lenses: "Tell Me What You See— Now Look Again"

"It should be one's sole endeavor to see everything afresh and create it anew."

—GUSTAV MAHLER

SOME OF MY FAVORITE CHILDHOOD MEMORIES include the trips our family took across the United States in an old motorhome. With a self-employed artist father and a K–12 educator mother, we had about two to three months each summer for either a trip to my mom's hometown of Kohala on the Big Island of Hawai'i or a motorhome trip. On these road trips, we'd stop at KOAs (Kampgrounds of America), park the motorhome, and stay a few nights before moving on to the next KOA in the neighboring state.

During one of these stops, when I was about seven or eight years old, my father decided to give me an art lesson—as he had done so many times before. We sat at the motorhome meal table (the size of half a card table) and looked out the window toward a beautiful Midwest landscape as I gathered my colored pencils. First, he instructed me to "look outside and tell me what you see." I looked and told him that I saw the mountains, the grass, trees, clouds, the sky, and an old building. He said, "OK . . . draw everything you see. When I look at your drawing, I want to feel like I'm looking out this window." I started drawing. My father was a fine artist and had painted numerous landscapes that adorned our home. I wanted to make him proud.

After sketching out basics of the landscape, I picked up the green colored pencil and started coloring in the grass.

"What are you doing?" my father asked. Caught off guard, I hesitantly told him I was coloring the grass. He said, "Look outside." I looked outside and then looked back at my father, still somewhat confused. He then said, "Now look again . . . what color is the grass?"

I looked outside and to my amazement, the grass was actually yellow. I said, "Yellow."

"YES," he enthusiastically said. "And what color is the sky?" I looked outside and before I could say, "Blue," I realized that the sky was somewhat orange. "What color are the mountains?" he continued. "Don't look at your paper, look outside."

As I looked at the mountains, my previous assumption of brown started to shift to purple. This process of looking outside and reaching for a different colored pencil went on for some time. I remember completing the drawing with all the new colors. I showed it to him, and he smiled and said, "That looks really great. Now, look again." By the time I had finished, the sunlight had shifted, and the colors had changed. My dad could tell that I now felt frustrated, and he quickly added, "You don't have to change anything to your drawing. It looks great. I just wanted you to see that the colors are always changing and that's a good thing. As an artist, it's more fun to paint the same scene with different lighting."

Throughout the process of writing this book, this particular memory came to mind over and over again. Over the past five years, as I experienced new things, learned from diverse individuals, and observed the changes in the world, I felt frustrated at times because the lighting of the landscape kept changing. Every day, I have felt like I have needed to continually refine my approach to humanity. Then I think of my father and what he would say to me. I imagine he would excitedly tell me that this book is great. And . . . there is so much more to learn and contribute because the lighting will change again. Then my mom would add a reminder that the need for kindness, compassion, and love never changes.

The Lenses of Humanity were never meant to be the solution to all of life's struggles and society's ills. They were meant to invite us to look . . . and then look again as often as we can. It is not only possible to develop these four lenses (Inner, Context, Empathy, and Community), it is imperative that we make every effort to do so if we are to elevate human dignity.

Humanity is not a destination; it is a journey. This journey invites continual growth. It requires intentional reflection and introspection to understand ourselves and one another better. It urges us to step out of our comfort zones and lean in to healthy dissonance. It calls for more intentional exposure to, education about, and engagement with difference. It challenges us to see the best in each other and give one another the benefit of the doubt. It asks for cultural humility, genuine inquiry, and courageous empathy. It invites us to build community with those who preceded us, those around us, and those who will follow us. This journey encourages us to do all we can to lift humanity. Through greater reflection, connection, and empathy, we can and will heal our world.

Notes

Introduction

1. "3.2 The Beginning of Theories & Models of Reflective Practice—John Dewey," Open Library, https://ecampusontario.pressbooks.pub /reflectivepracticeinearlyyears/chapter/3-2-beginning-theories/.

2. Robert Waldinger and Marc Shulz, *The Good Life: Lessons from the World's Longest Scientific Study of Happiness* (New York: Simon & Schuster, 2022).

Chapter 1

1. "Skin-to-Skin Contact," Intermountain Health, accessed May 1, 2024, https://intermountainhealthcare.org/about/transforming-healthcare /innovation/clinical-programs/women-and-newborns/skin-to -skin-contact/.

2. "Baby's Brain Begins Now: Conception to Age 3," The Urban Child Institute, accessed May 1, 2024, http://www.urbanchildinstitute.org /why-0-3/baby-and-brain.

3. All participants of my focus groups lived in the United States and the majority self-identified as US citizens.

4. Caroline Mala Corbin, "Terrorists Are Always Muslim but Never White: At the Intersection of Critical Race Theory and Propaganda," *Fordham Law Review* 86, no. 2 (2017): https://ir.lawnet.fordham.edu/flr/vol86/iss2/5/.

Chapter 2

1. Pierre Bourdieu, "The Forms of Capital," in *Handbook of Theory and Research for the Sociology of Education*, ed. John G. Richardson (Westport, CT: Greenwood, 1986): 241–258.

2. The term Hispanic is used in reference to individuals who self-identify with origins from Latin American countries or who identify as Latina, Latino, or Latinx.

3. Kenneth Clark and Mamie Clark, "Emotional Factors in Racial Identification and Preference in Negro Children," in *Readings in Social Psychology*, eds. Theodore Newcomb and Eugene Hartley (New York: Holt, 1947): 169–178.

4. Claude Steele, *Whistling Vivaldi: How Stereotypes Affect Us and What We Can Do* (New York: WW. Norton & Co, 2010).

5. The Characteristic Map is a variation of an exercise I was introduced to by Dr. Bryan Waite and Dr. Mike Patch, faculty members in the School of Education at Utah Valley University.

Chapter 4

1. Chimamanda Ngozi Adichie, "Danger of a Single Story," TED Talks, July 2009, https://www.ted.com/talks/chimamanda_ngozi_adichie _the_danger_of_a_single_story?language=en.

2. "Who Writes History?" *Business Recorder*, February 4, 2017, https:// www.brecorder.com/news/4473619.

Chapter 5

1. "The Importance of Bedside Manner," David Geffen School of Medicine, UCLA, July 16, 2016, https://medschool.ucla.edu/blog-post/the -importance-of-bedside-manner.

Chapter 6

1. Michael Dimock and Richard Wike, "America Is Exceptional in the Nature of Its Political Divide," Pew Research Center, November 13, 2020, https://www.pewresearch.org/fact-tank/2020/11/13/america-is -exceptional-in-the-nature-of-its-political-divide/.

Chapter 8

1. Tamara Glenz, "The Importance of Learning Students' Names," *Journal on Best Teaching Practices* (April 2014): http://teachingonpurpose.org /wp-content/uploads/2015/03/Glenz-T.-2014.-The-importance-of -learning-students-names.pdf.

2. Joyce Russell, "Career Coach: The Power of Using a Name," *The Washington Post*, January 12, 2014, https://www.washingtonpost.com /business/capitalbusiness/career-coach-the-power-of-using-a-name /2014/01/10/8ca03da0-787e-11e3-8963-b4b654bcc9b2_story/.

3. Karen Sternheimer, "The Importance of Knowing Names," *Everyday Sociology*, blog, January 17, 2014, https://www.everydaysociologyblog .com/2014/01/the-importance-of-knowing-names.html.

4. Jennifer Stanchfield, "The Importance of Names," *Experiential Tools*, blog, September 2, 2013, https://blog.experientialtools.com/2013 /09/02/the-importance-of-names/.

5. Albert Mehrabian and Suan Ferris, "Inference of Attitudes from Nonverbal Communication in Two Channels," *Journal of Consulting Psychology* 31, no. 3 (1967): 248–252.

Chapter 9

1. "Who Was Whitney Young?," Whitney M. Young Magnet School, accessed May 1, 2024, https://wyoung.org/m/pages/index.jsp?uREC _ID=256701&type=d.

Chapter 11

1. Robert Putnam, *Our Kids: The American Dream in Crisis* (New York: Simon & Schuster, 2015).

2. Henry Mintzberg, "Rebuilding Companies as Communities," *Harvard Business Review*, July–August 2009, https://hbr.org/2009/07/rebuilding -companies-as-communities.

3. Robert Putnam, *Bowling Alone: The Collapse and Revival of American Community* (New York: Simon & Schuster, 2000).

Chapter 12

1. In 2020, Cigna conducted a national survey of over 10,000 US adults and compared the results to their 2018 survey of 20,000 adults. Cigna, *Loneliness and the Workplace*, 2020, https://legacy.cigna.com/static /www-cigna-com/docs/about-us/newsroom/studies-and-reports /combatting-loneliness/cigna-2020-loneliness-report.pdf.

2. Amy Novotney, "The Risks of Social Isolation," *Monitor on Psychology* 50, no. 5 (May 2019), https://www.apa.org/monitor/2019/05/ce -corner-isolation.

3. Jody Schoenecker, "Loneliness and Our Health," Welia Health, September 9, 2021, https://www.weliahealth.org/2021/09 /loneliness-and-our-health/.

4. Melissa Hunt, Rachel Marx, Courtney Lispon, and Jordyn Young, "No More FOMO: Limiting Social Media Decreases Loneliness and Depression," *Journal of Social and Clinical Psychology* 37, no. 10 (December 2018).

About the Author

Photo by Skye Johansen

DR. KYLE A. REYES currently serves as vice president of Institutional Advancement at Utah Valley University (UVU)—the largest university in the state of Utah. During his twenty-one years at UVU, Kyle has worked as VP of Student Affairs, chief inclusion officer, chief of staff to the president, and a variety of outreach and student support roles. Kyle is also a tenured associate professor of education. His research and courses focus on multicultural education, cross-cultural communication, family and community partnerships, and arts-based integration. Kyle has consulted with, and given more than seven hundred presentations to, organizations in over thirty states and Canada in various sectors, including K–12 education, higher education, business, community, and faith groups.

Kyle serves on the board of Asian Pacific Americans in Higher Education and was president of the Utah chapter of the National Association for Multicultural Education. He has also served as the co-chair of the College Access Network for the Utah System of

Higher Education and a member of the board of directors for the United Way of Utah County and American Indian Services. Kyle has received a number of awards, including the Exemplary Educator for Diversity Award from the National Association of Multicultural Education (NAME), Inclusion Cultivates Excellence Award from CUPA-HR, *Utah Valley Magazine*'s Top 40 Under 40, and the Top 50 Diversity Executives in the Nation from *Diversity MBA Magazine*. Kyle received his PhD in educational leadership and policy from the University of Utah and was the recipient of the Bennion Morgan Fellowship. Kyle lives with his wife, Michele, and their seven children in Vineyard, Utah. Together, they enjoy sports, travel, and the development of artistic expression and celebration connected to their Hawaiian, Navajo, Filipino, and Japanese heritages.

Made in United States
Troutdale, OR
12/04/2024

25921485R00128